NO EMPLOYMENT LAWYER REQUIRED

STEPHANIE ROBINSON
(Chartered CIPD)

ISBN-13: 978-1-5272-3436-9

DEDICATION

To Dad for my passion for business, to Mum for instilling her resilience and determination in me and for Grace, for love and always.

CONTENTS

ACKNOWLEDGMENTS

Thanks goes to the Solve HR team for continuing to believe in our mission to solve clients' problems in a pragmatic, fair and compliant way and working hard to build and retain excellent client relationships. Thanks also to Mark Grint, editor, for his enthusiastic support, counselling and dedication to this project.

INTRODUCTION

Many SME businesses today are retaining lawyers and HR professionals to help them navigate the complex world of employment law. This can be time-consuming and costly, but business owners are resorting to this because they simply do not have complete confidence in their ability to manage people. The old adage, *'you don't know what you don't know'* applies, and that opens the gate to you and your business being exploited by advisors and zealous employees. Therefore, my reason for writing this book is to share what I've learned in my own experience, to demystify the employment landscape, and to arm you, the SME owner, with the knowledge and insight to gain that confidence.

When you go into business, I fully appreciate that you're putting your heart and soul into it. I know this because I have done it myself. You are the one taking the risks, and yet oftentimes employees appear to be taking advantage of your vulnerabilities. This book is written with an appreciation and understanding of your commitment, concerns and challenges and with the aim of supporting you in making sure your business succeeds. I will reference some real life business owner mistakes because I firmly believe in learning from your mistakes, or better still, the mistakes of others wherever possible. Why should you have to learn everything from scratch just because you are a new business owner? This book is intended to be a short-cut and cost-effective guide to minimising the pitfalls when you employ people. Each chapter ends with a summary that you can refer back to time and time again.

Additionally, my hope is that you will gain a solid foundation of employment law that enables you to confidently make decisions about your business, its people and its structure. Moreover, I hope it enables you to grow your company effectively, without undue people-related setbacks and without facing inordinately expensive advisor bills.

All the best.

1

DISMISSING SAFELY AND THE BASICS OF EMPLOYMENT LAW

AFTER great consideration, I am going to unapologetically launch into dismissals in the very first chapter. If you're picking up this book you have probably already tried the 'softer', 'policy, engagement, culture' approaches but one particular individual or recurring scenario has left you at a loss as to your options. You are perhaps recognising that some uncomfortable action may have to be taken. So let's get started with what you can do as dismissing a member of staff today seems to be, in many people's perception, quite an easy action to take if required, mainly because there is the opportunity to capitalise on the two-year short-service dismissal rule and legislation.

However before we go into that, I'd like to talk about the four underpinning pieces of legislation which should shape all of your hiring-and-firing-related decisions. Without trying to lecture here (as I bet a lecture is not why you've picked up this book) it would help you to be aware of the four different pillars of employment legislation in the UK today. They are things your employment lawyer will probably never tell you, so here they described in a simple, straightforward way:

- Statute law
- Contractual law
- Custom and practice
- Case legislation

The four forms of Employment legislation.

Employment legislation comes in four forms: firstly, there is statute law. Statutes are legislative instruments that come from Whitehall or from the EU. In the United Kingdom and most of Europe, we make our own laws, and up until recently were also required to implement European directives as a member of the European Union. In many cases it has been agreed that a certain level of discretion can be used in how directives are applied in the UK, hence why we have things like the working hours directive 'opt-out'.

Secondly there is contractual law. You'll most likely be familiar with the term, 'breach of contract' so, where a written contract exists – also known as an explicit contract – in commercial or employment law terms, if you fail to act in line with the terms stipulated within that contract then it has effectively been breached. Yet this can also apply to an implied agreement, meaning an agreement which has formed over time, in effect, by the continuance of routine business activity and a breach to an implied contract can happen when you do not behave in line with the spirit of that implied contract.

Thirdly, please note that what is written in black and white in a contract can be superseded by an implied agreement i.e. your company's custom and practice. For example, if you have stated the hours of work in your explicit contract of employment as 9:00am-5:00pm Monday to Friday, yet you've asked the employee to change their hours of work to 8:00am-4:00pm for a couple of weeks but this then continues for a period of six months or more, those amended hours are normally presumed to be the new contractual terms, forming a new 'implicit contract' between the parties. Custom and practice have altered the contract and, for the avoidance of doubt, an employment tribunal would be likely to consider the latest agreed working pattern to be the contracted working hours, regardless of what is written in black and white in the original document. Custom and practice, therefore, is like a formula for deciding what the existing terms of a contract are when nothing has been written down in black and white. I have come across many cases where an agreement was reached but nothing was followed up in writing – in these (fairly common) cases 'custom and practice' is then relied upon to inform how a contract should be perceived and construed. For example, in these cases, if I were to ask a new client the following questions and get the following answers:

Q: What day do you pay staff?
A: Monday.
Q: How do you pay your staff?
A: Into their bank, by cheque.
Q: What hours do staff work?
A: Monday to Friday 9:00am to 5:00pm for office staff, but the site staff work 8:00am to 4.30pm.

...then these would form the terms of the contract of employment. This is important because, if there was a dispute or you or wanted to change a work practice and the staff weren't happy about it, a tribunal judge would always first look at what was happening materially, in practice, in the workplace, and consider the evidence for the existing practice being the status quo. There would then be a judgement on whether or not any changes that you enforced as an employer, or any changes the employee tried to make, were in fact a breach of the implied contract between the parties, as construed through custom and practice.

The other source of legislation that your business is subject to when making employment decisions is case legislation. Case legislation is exactly what it says on the tin. When a tribunal result has been defined it creates case law. In some cases the topic being considered or the process being reviewed and the subsequent judgement made upon it creates a precedent for how employment law should be applied to workplaces. As a result, statute law may then be created to codify this outcome and make a practice or process become a legal requirement for employers to follow.

A recent example of how case law now shapes the employment landscape is a set of judgements made last year on holiday payments for those on regular commission and overtime. This was previously a grey area, as the law did not specify rules on holiday payments due in the case of ongoing regular 'top-up' earnings. Two separate individuals questioned what they should receive when on annual leave: one regularly received commission payments throughout the year and the other regularly (almost every day) received a payment for overtime. The practice had been that their respective employers only paid them a basic rate when they were on holiday. The complainants argued that as they routinely (every month) received their commission or overtime payments as pay for work conducted, it had become custom and therefore implied in their contracts' of employment that this was their monthly pay. Accordingly, they should continue to receive basic plus commission or payment for overtime when on holiday. The employers argued that the employee, being on holiday, was unable to actually earn commission or overtime because they were not present and were not making sales. Naturally one might agree that the employer's position makes sense, however the separate judges favoured the employee's arguments: that as the commission and overtime had come to be relied upon and it had become part of their regular remuneration it should be continued to be paid when on holiday.

The possibility of ending up in this predicament should be considered in any calculations or offer an employer is making when revising pay. Fortunately, where unlawful deductions of wages claims can go back as many as six years, claims of this nature were capped at two years as otherwise it could have meant many companies being put out of business as a result of these two landmark decisions. So case law can be pretty complicated.

Clearly there is the need to get to the crux of the judgement, and look at how it would apply to your workforce. There are many companies in the UK that operate with the approach that because it's not in statute, they ignore what the case law says. In particular, where judgements are particularly unfavourable or 'un-economic', normally in relation to working time and minimum wage: for example, judgements applied to 'sleep-in' working arrangements often found in the care industry. In this example care providers may choose not pay for every hour an employee 'sleeps in' in a client/patient home, because if the employee is sleeping, they're not working, despite being 'on-call'. However, a judgement considered the sleeping time to still be 'working time' and thus payable.

As an adviser to many companies we regularly stay on top of case law and make sure our employers or businesses understand the implications of case legislation. A past case judgement is likely to be the judgement that would be relied upon if one of your employees was to take you to court for the same or similar reason, and hence, although it's not written in statute, it's good practice to update your policies and procedures to reflect case judgements. For example: recently it was decided that travel time between a job should be considered as work time; this is where the workforce have a number of appointments at different locations throughout the day. Now the time spent travelling to each location will need to be covered as 'work time' and should be paid at least at the National Minimum Wage rate. A supplementary payment, or no payment, or just payment for fuel, is not acceptable; the employee should be paid at their normal rate.

However, some businesses may feel that they cannot implement this and choose to ignore this judgement due to the resulting cost to their payroll. And you can, of course, choose to ignore judgements and many employers do have legitimate reasons for doing this:

- The judgement may not fully apply to their business as it only touches on a small part of the working arrangement.
- They can't afford to apply it.
- They take the view that statute may water down the requirements from the case once incorporated into an Act.
- The case is being appealed and they will only apply the judgement when it has been ratified by The European Court of Justice (we will have to wait and see, but likely to be the Court of Appeal in the future for the United Kingdom post Brexit.)

So those are the four facets that constitute employment law. But how does this all affect a business when dismissing an employee?

Short Service Dismissals – dismissals for employees with less than two years' service.

The law presently allows you to dismiss an employee with under two years' service without following the full ACAS Code of Practice procedures and thus prevents them from raising a tribunal claim for unfair dismissal. However… your own contracts of employment may not! You must have a provision in your contract that allows you to dismiss an employee with under two-year's service, otherwise you will likely fall foul of a breach of contract claim. You should reserve your company's right not to follow your full company disciplinary procedure. Otherwise you could be in breach of your own contract and your own terms and conditions.

So what are you bypassing and/or gaining, if you do reserve your company's right to capitalise on the two year short service dismissal legislation? The law presently means that an employer can dismiss an vith less than two-year's service without been tied to ..g the ACAS Code of Practice for dismissals, which is required where service is greater than two years. This Code of Practice can be a convoluted process because normally it requires the employer to follow at least a two or three step prescribed process as a minimum, as outlined below – note that many companies and organisations make the process even more complex through their own policies:

- The process normally requires an investigation (conducting a thorough and reasonable investigation is discussed below). On conclusion of the investigation, the next step is to formally invite the employee to a meeting to which they have the right to be accompanied, giving them appropriate notice.
- Step two is to have the meeting and listen to their representations. A decision is then taken and should be followed up in writing, allowing the employee to appeal, should they wish, any decision taken against them.

The above would be the normal minimum process that the law would require for a gross misconduct dismissal decision to be legal. However, the unfair dismissal legislation allows you to waive this for staff with less than two years and potentially, in the worst case scenario, bring somebody in without warning and tell them that they're terminated. But hang fire on firing please!

How not to fall foul of the rules when capitalising on Short Service legislation.

Despite removing the risk of a tribunal for unfair dismissal for employees with less than two years' service, there are still a number of risks that you can be exposing your business to as there are other statutory instruments, in particular the 2010 Equality Act (which tied together all the strands of discrimination legislation) which give employees 'Day One rights'. These are protections afforded pre-employment, under legislation for protection from discrimination in these areas: sexual, marital status, gender reassignment, sexual orientation, age, disability, race, religion, caste; it also offers protection from health and safety grievances and protection from any grievance or request related to requiring an employer to follow their statutory obligations, often referred to as an employee 'asserting' their statutory rights. An example of assertion of statutory rights is the protection afforded to an employee if they raise a grievance about working without a break or if they thought their aggregate pay was below the National Minimum Wage. In short, it grants protection to employees for enforcing their legal rights.

To bring this to life: you hire somebody and chose to pay them a weekly rate. Within two weeks of them working with you, they say, "You know the weekly rate you pay me? When I divide it by the 60 hours of work that you're asking me to work, it means that my hourly rate is below the National Minimum Wage (NMW) and I would therefore like my salary, or my weekly wage, to be increased to reflect my legal entitlement to be paid the National Living/Minimum hourly rate." Alternatively, they may say "Keep the amount that you pay me constant, but I'll work less hours so the hourly rate is effectively equal to the NMW rate."

If you subsequently refused their claim and then later dismissed them *(not that you would, because you will have read this book!)* or they walked out when you failed to do anything about it and subsequently claimed that you constructively dismissed them then they would still be entitled to bring a claim to an employment tribunal, despite not having two years' service with your company. In this example the individual would likely have claims for constructive/unfair dismissal and unlawful deductions of pay. In statistics published by the government for awards relating to unfair dismissal, in 2016/2017 (numbers are rounded) the maximum award was £1.7m, the median award was £7.5k and the average award was £16.5k*.

This 'assertation of statutory rights' can apply to a number of other scenarios including Health and Safety, whistleblowing and Trade Union membership or activity. For example if a dismissed employee is a trade union representative (whether your business has a trade union or not), and they felt that they were dismissed after an earlier issue relating to their membership and/or involvement in the union, even if the dismissal is six months down the line, then if you fail to give a good alternative reason for their dismissal, they could infer the dismissal was in fact related to their association with the union. In this case, the onus falls on you as the employer to show that their dismissal was not for union-related activities, and for a tribunal to then decide if they believe your excuses.

* https://www.gov.uk/government/statistics/tribunals-and-gender-recognition-certificate-statistics-quarterly-april-to-june-2017-and-2016-to-2017

In addition, there are many individual characteristics that are protected under the Equality Act. For example, the Equality Act allows for protection from discrimination by association and perception. Discrimination by association is best illustrated by imagining a case where an employee is required to care for a disabled relative and they are dismissed immediately after their genuine request to allow some changes to their working hours primarily in order to take their relative to the hospital regularly.

Dyslexia is often not seen as a disability in today's society; however, because the definition of disability changed in the Equality Act of 2010, disability is no longer defined by a catalogue of specified illnesses and conditions. The Equality Act definition now focuses on how the life of an individual in routine day-to-day activities is affected. Such as, can they walk and climb stairs? Can they get up from bed and wash and clothe themselves? Can they lift regular day to day items? Can they feed themselves? The definition is very wide now, to the extent that recently pre-menstrual syndrome, (yes, even PMS!) was considered a disability by a tribunal! The impact of this wide definition is that it is quite straightforward for an employee to demonstrate that they might be disabled in some way and are therefore protected.

So, the long and short of it is, that you still need to take time and care with dismissals. Otherwise, you could dismiss somebody in their probationary period for lateness or poor attitude, but instead the employee believes their dismissal was related to their race, sex, a request for leave or any other protected reason; this would make them eligible to go to a tribunal and make a claim on these grounds. Scarily, discrimination penalties are uncapped and so you are exposed to legal costs and a pay-out of potentially thousands of pounds in compensation and fines.

If the thought of an expensive tribunal pay-out is not enough to hammer home the idea that going straight for the jugular with a short service dismissal is not always a good idea, consider this, employees still have protections, even before they've been hired!

When you are accepting applications to hire in your business, you are legally bound to make a fair selection and not discriminate in the process. There was a case years ago where an Asian gentleman applied to one organisation for a secretarial and administration role; he had relevant experience and his CV was well-constructed, but he had an Asian name. When he wasn't getting much success in the job market he applied to the same organisation again but this time he thought that he would experiment. He changed his name to a typical white British female name; the employer immediately invited him – her, his pseudonym – for an interview. In his subsequent employment tribunal claim for discrimination on the basis of sex and race, he was able to show that his experience on both CV's was almost identical and therefore it must be that his identity as an Asian man that was the reason why he wasn't invited to an interview. He successfully brought a claim against the prospective employer for racial and sex discrimination, and the judgement required the company to pay him £5,000 in compensation. Note, he hadn't even worked a day for them!

The same man did this several times more, earning around £20,000 by suing various businesses who clearly could be shown in court to have discriminatory recruitment practices. So please take this as a warning and look at making your recruitment practices robust, briefing employees who are involved in your recruitment process on the dangers of poor selection. This is explored in **Chapter 8: Recruiting the best.**

Getting on with a Short Service Dismissal.

Now you understand that there are dangers from not considering 'day one rights' however, are you still left wondering how the best way is to mitigate against these pitfalls and still make a dismissal. So, these might be your circumstances:

- You realise that your new employee has the wrong attitude.
- You are convinced there are no risks from discrimination or assertion of statutory rights and wish to press on with an immediate termination for someone with less than two years.

We'll look first at holding a meeting with the employee when you do not wish to write to them about it first. So what do you do?

1. Prepare for the meeting:
   a) Decide where and when you are going to meet with the employee. Pick the best time, ideally, end of the day or start of the day, if you prefer.

   b) Check the contract of employment and notice period:
      - Calculate the difference between their start date and their proposed termination date given the relevant notice period (either as stated in the contract or if there is no contract, the statutory entitlement, a week's notice for every of service) to ensure this does not take them over two years' service and hence require you follow the full legal process outlined below.
      - Decide if you will pay in lieu of notice or ask them to work their notice. What might soften the blow and protect your company reputation? For example, paying an extra week or month of notice?
   c) Consider restrictive covenants and/or confidentiality clauses and enforcing these.
   d) Check if there is any outstanding holiday pay owed/accrued.
   e) Check if any other monies are owed to the company or by the company, for example waiving training agreements.
   f) Consider company property (cars, laptop) and keys and what you are going to ask of the employee in relation to these.
   g) Decide when to switch off access to systems.

2. Ask your employee to join you, and ideally another colleague who can take notes.
3. If the employee asks to be accompanied at the meeting, allow them to bring in a willing colleague to the meeting. In this case, explain to the colleague they are there to support the employee and cannot answer questions on their colleague's behalf.
4. Explain to them the reasons for the meeting and what action you are considering, namely their dismissal.
5. Focus on the facts and behaviours that have led you to this point. Try to depersonalise it. For example:
   a) Lateness on four occasions.
   b) Lack of understanding of the systems, despite their answers at interview which led you to believe they were competent in those systems.
   c) Failing to fit in to the culture and work with colleagues,

dispute with finance team and office manager, where you have satisfied yourself these disputes could have been handled better on their account.

d) Failing to deliver to results or targets.

6. Ask them for their thoughts on your statements with regards to their performance or the issues you identified. If they are truly shocked and unprepared, let them take their time and collect their thoughts.
7. If the meeting gets heated, adjourn and take a short break.
8. If they don't say anything of material importance in their defence then you are normally safe to confirm your decision to dismiss and can then discuss:
   a) Notice period.
   b) Any payments.
   c) Follow up.
9. Although not legally required, it can be a good idea to offer an appeal avenue to an employee, particularly if the dismissal was very unexpected or quickly executed. This can help mitigate and prevent any tribunal claims on the basis of 'day one rights' as outlined above and shows you are committed to a fair process even in short service dismissals.
10. You could have a letter ready to hand confirming to the employee the decision to dismiss, outlining the above items in nine and 10 above, though be aware this could infer the decision was a fait accompli or premediated. And to err on the side of caution, you could have another letter ready to extend the probation or give the employee a reprieve by a further six to eight weeks.
11. As you are most exposed to a tribunal claim or a claim of an infringement of 'day one rights' if no written or verbally recorded reason was given for their dismissal, I encourage you to follow up any termination in writing stating the reasons for the termination.

Now we'll look at holding a meeting where you do first write to the employee about the meeting. If you feel that this 'surprise meeting' which is likely to end in dismissal will be too much for the employee or is unfair, perhaps because there have been no pervious performance conversations, then the alternative is to invite the employee to the meeting in advance, outlining the particular points of poor performance/attitude that you will be discussing. In this letter * you should include wording to make it clear that the employee's continued employment is being considered and they could be terminated as a result of the meeting. You should also reference your company's contractual right not to follow the full disciplinary or capability procedure because of the employee's short service. The steps after this are mostly similar to points 1-11 above, ignoring any that points that reference holding the meeting with no notice.

How to dismiss employees with two years' service or more.
As alluded to earlier, dismissing employees who have worked for you for over two years can be more complicated. The ACAS Code of Practice requires a fair process and that employers follow at least the following steps for both disciplinary and grievance proceedings:

1. Employers and employees should raise and deal with issues promptly and should not delay meetings, decisions or confirmation of those decisions unreasonably.
2. Employers and employees should act consistently.
3. Employers should carry out any necessary investigations, to establish the facts of the case.
4. Employers should inform employees of the basis of the problem and give them an opportunity to put their case in response before any decisions are made.
5. Employers should allow employees to be accompanied at any formal disciplinary or grievance meeting.
6. Employers should allow an employee to appeal against any formal decision made.

After an employee's service of two years or more, employers are expected to follow these guidelines if looking to dismiss. The extra length of service means there are more hoops to jump through if the employee is suspected of misconduct, gross or otherwise or is just not performing to the standards required. Even then, following the process alone does not always guarantee a safe dismissal, because a tribunal will be looking to determine an organisation's reasonableness, not only in their process which led to the dismissal decision, but also in the reasonableness of the decision itself.

The following process should be considered:

- Make sure you note all the early statements made at the time of discovery or immediately after the incident, in particular by the accused. This should be passed on to any investigator.

- Decide if you need to conduct an investigation to determine if there is firstly a case to answer. This may be bypassed where the case is cut and dry and/or the employee has admitted misconduct. However not all cases are immediately clear or straightforward.
- Consideration should be then given to whether or not the employee of the alleged offence should be suspended. Normally suspension will be appropriate:
  a) To protect the evidence and witnesses.
  b) To protect other employees and/or the accused.
  c) If the offence is likely to be gross misconduct. Having the employee continue working at your business, with access to equipment and material may pose too great a risk.

Suspension should not be used as a punitive measure or to imply a foregone conclusion and this should normally be reinforced in any suspension letter. Also the employee should be paid fully during any suspension period.

Investigations – if required.

Should an investigation be required then it is worth following these steps:

- Appoint a thorough, detail-orientated investigator (or team of two if you can) almost immediately after any incident or suspected misconduct has been determined. These investigators should be impartial and not involved in the incident or be a witness to the incident. It can be a line manager of the employee, provided the manager was not already a witness or a party to the incident. If your business is small you might consider asking your accountant, a non-executive director or a HR consultant.
- The investigators should start the investigation by talking to the accused and taking a statement detailing their story and explanations. It might be that after differing witness statements and new evidence, the investigators go back to the accused employee and ask further questions. They should also reference the earliest statements made around the time of the incident or discovery.
- The investigators should look at the disciplinary policy in your company and determine the process and principles they are

required to follow. Importantly they should also identify where the allegation(s) apply in the list of offences listed in the disciplinary policy.

- If the allegations are complex, with lots of evidence, screen shots, witness statements, images, evidence of messages then the investigators should compile a report of the investigation. A typical report might include the following types of information:
    a) The circumstances and allegations.
    b) The process/steps the investigation has taken, and why.
    c) The evidence list and witness statements by page and corresponding evidence.
    d) A conclusion which relates to the offences and disciplinary policy/standards of the company and importantly a conclusion to whether there is a case to answer or not.
    e) Recommendations, normally for a disciplinary hearing and/or other action, for example, training, imposing new standards, discussions with other employees, security information.

It's worth noting that the aim and test of a good investigation done properly, is one where in the event of a disciplinary hearing, the disciplinary Chair has little to do other than to hear the employee's excuses and consider these with the investigation findings and any other precedent for action in the company.

Disciplinary hearings.

Where allegations are complex and the findings of the investigation recommend a disciplinary hearing or where the case is straightforward with easily collated evidence that clearly points to having a disciplinary hearing, then the next step is to invite the accused to the disciplinary hearing. An invitation to a disciplinary hearing should:

- Identify the time and date for the hearing, which should be at least 48 hours after the employee will receive their invitation letter – but remember 'reasonableness' will be the test any employment tribunal will consider so the minimum of 48 hours may be extended if the employee requests an extension and non-working days don't count so a Friday invitation for a Monday meeting would be considered unreasonable.

- Outline the allegations.
- Include all evidence and any investigation report to support the allegations.
- Identify who will chair the disciplinary hearing, ensuring that they have not been part of the investigation or the incident.
- Give the employee the right to be accompanied to the hearing by a fellow colleague or trade union representative (see the section below entitled "Can an employee be accompanied to a disciplinary hearing")
- If the allegations being considered are for gross misconduct, you must state that in the invitation letter. If it is decided the employee did commit gross misconduct, one potential outcome could be dismissal.
- Reference your company disciplinary policy and include it in the information sent to the employee.

In terms of running the disciplinary hearing, preparation is key. The Chair (which might be you, and will be referenced as such in the following paragraph) must keep an open mind, not jumping to conclusions, and be prepared to be fair and thorough. Ensure that you have read through all the notes, the investigation report and have formulated your questions or have a script to follow to ensure you don't lose your train of thought. If anything does not make sense or you have more questions for the investigator, ideally ask them in advance sharing the responses with the employee, or have the investigator on hand for the disciplinary hearing.

Ensure you have a note-taker present to take notes of the hearing. At the end of the meeting, it is good practice for the note-taker to take the attendees through their notes and gain agreement on the written record. The notes should then be sent out after the hearing to all parties by the minute taker; the disciplinary decision may be sent with these notes or separately afterwards. This can be done by email and I recommend asking parties to read and respond with any corrections by a defined deadline. Normally recording hearings is not permitted, however, the Chair can take a view of whether this is appropriate.

As the Chair your role is to listen to the employee and their representations first and foremost and then reach a decision on behalf of the company. In doing so it is key to hear the employee's side and probe any explanations or excuses in a non-confrontational way. It is worth starting any disciplinary hearing with the employee's statements – I often read these aloud. This firstly shows you have heard and taken cognisance of the employee's point of view and version of events and a written statement is often easier to follow and refer back to as the hearing progresses. You can of course then ask them if they have anything to add, which they probably will, having seen the witness statements/evidence. It is worth noting any points of contention in the stories and then evaluating how important these points are. You can often get waylaid by the 'he-said-she-said' and if it makes no material difference to the misconduct, then focus back on the actions that are central to the misconduct.

At no time should the Chair, or others in the room, be confrontational or judgemental. The Chair is responsible for setting the tone of the meeting and if you make it clear early on that you consider the hearing to be a professional meeting where all are expected to behave professionally and outline everyone's role this can make the meeting go smoother. Naturally, employees will be anxious and excited and may arrive animated for the hearing. The Chair should remind the employee that the Chair's role is to ensure a fair hearing and that if things get heated an adjournment may be called. I often suggest to the employee and their representative in my opening remarks that they can also call an adjournment should they wish to.

Allowing an employee to be accompanied at a disciplinary hearing.

The law allows for an employee to be accompanied by a fellow colleague or trade union representative. Your organisation does not need to recognise a union for the employee to bring a trade union representative into a formal meeting. They can be a member independently of a union or indeed might not even be a member yet they can still have a representative to accompany them. You can legitimately ask any union representative for identification to confirm they are an elected representative.

Often we are asked if a mother or friend or lawyer can accompany an employee in a hearing. Our advice is to stick to your policy and only permit colleagues or union representation as the legislation affords. If an employee has learning or disability challenges or is younger than 18 then it may be sensible to allow that companion to attend to make the process easier all round – it may be even considered a reasonable

adjustment for someone who has been off sick with stress.
If an employee does arrive for a meeting with a companion, the Chair's role is to outline that the companion may speak in the hearing and support the employee – they may even wish to take notes – but that any question directed at the employee should be answered by the employee.

Making a disciplinary decision.
Ordinarily, decisions should not be made during a disciplinary hearing – even a brief adjournment is a good idea before making and communicating a decision. The adjournment should be used to review notes and also check understanding with the hearing's note-taker. Disciplinary decisions should be made by the Chair of the hearing and not by HR or a note-taker.

Following the process is one thing; making the decision however, can be difficult. An employment tribunal's guiding principle in judging if a dismissal was fair, is not just whether or not they followed the prescribed process, but they also consider whether an employer has acted reasonably in their decision to dismiss. This means any Chair has to consider mitigating factors that the employee puts forward and those that the investigation uncovers. These can include, but are not limited to, years of service without a warning or issues, lack of understanding on the gravity of their actions, apologies and/or acceptance of wrong-doing, poor management practices.

Equally the Chair may have to consider precedents of other employees who have faced similar charges or who have previously been disciplined. Note, you are not required to follow a previous precedent to the letter or to take a blanket approach; in fact, tribunals do appreciate a more considered approach. For example, an employee who has three years' service and was perceived to be ambivalent to allegations could be dismissed and yet someone with 20 years' service who was particularly remorseful could be issued with a final written warning and suspension without pay as a penalty for gross misconduct.

In making the decision, Chairs are required to determine what level of 'misconduct' the employee has committed, if any. Gross misconduct can result in summary dismissal, which means dismissal without payment of notice pay. Serious misconduct could still result in dismissal after a series of warnings – however, there is a requirement to pay the employee for notice. You can exercise your pay in lieu of notice clause to pay them so they are not required to work their notice. Normally the outcomes available from a disciplinary hearing are the following:

- No warning and no action
- No warning but training or other measures
- First written warning also known as a verbal written warning – normally placed on an employee's record for three to six months, depending on your policy.
- Second written warning or a formal written warning – normally placed on an employee's record for nine to twelve months, depending on your policy.
- First and final written warning – normally placed on an employee's record for twelve months, depending on your policy. You might issue this 'first and final warning' where an employee has had no previous record, but the misconduct is serious enough to make it clear that any further breaches may result in dismissal.
- Final written warning. Normally placed on the record for 12 months.
- Dismissal with notice.
- Dismissal with no notice payment.
- Action short of dismissal, if your disciplinary policy affords for this, such as:
  a) Suspension with no pay – normally up to the equivalent period that a notice period would have been.
  b) Demotion.

Once the decision has been made and you have reconvened the meeting, you should give reasons explaining how you have arrived at the decision and any penalties, if applicable. Also explain the timescales for any warnings issued and state the employee's right of appeal and timescales and persons involved in appealing. These points should all be followed up formally in a letter issued to the employee. Any warning and timescales related to appeals will normally start from when the employee is in receipt of the letter, not the re-adjournment of the meeting or verbal communication of the outcome. The appeals procedure should accompany the letter as an enclosure or be copied and pasted. The minutes, ideally typed up or legible minutes, of the disciplinary hearing should also be enclosed.

Please note, this is the only legitimate process to give a formal warning to an employee which will be counted as valid by an employment tribunal. We still often hear managers say, 'I gave them a verbal warning'. Pulling a member of staff aside for a dressing down or even following up a conversation in an email does not count. It can be useful for you to refer to these in any later formal process; however, they do not count as any stage in the warning process which might ultimately lead to a dismissal.

Handling appeals.

In an ideal world an appeal hearing will be based on an employee's well considered written statements outlining the basis of their appeal – in reality this doesn't often happen. Oftentimes employees use it as an avenue for their case to be reviewed again. Always hear an appeal, because an appeal is enshrined in the ACAS Code of Practice, even if the reasons for the appeal are not clear.

During the appeal it is important that the appeal officer/chair tries to establish exactly what the employee is appealing against and only evaluate this. It may be the process taken, evidence that the decision was based on, or even alleged bias of the disciplinary chair. This is the initial part of the appeal process and concludes by making a decision regarding whether the appeal is successful or not. Following the appeal meeting, the findings of the appeal need to then be conveyed to the employee. You may choose to do the latter in an appeal outcome letter or, and I can hear you groan, you might have a follow-up meeting. Use your wisdom in terms of what you think the employee might accept and if there is anything to be gained from taking the time to explain to the employee in a face-to-face manner. Sometimes this maybe a waste of time given the employee's mind-set; on other occasions where the employee is staying with you or has made a well-argued appeal, then a follow-up meeting is a good investment in time.

Nevertheless, appeal hearings should be heard by someone different to the initial disciplinary manager, and ideally someone more senior in the organisation. If you are a small business and from the investigation and the disciplinary hearing you have exhausted your options of personnel able or available to hear the appeal you might consider asking your accountant, a non-executive director or a consultant. Failing that and provided your appeal policy states it, you can use the same manager/person who was the disciplinary Chair, however, you will probably have to show a tribunal that you exhausted all options first. This is a particularly risky strategy if the appeal is against the disciplinary chair's bias or approach.

The outcome from an appeal could be the following:

- Appeal dismissed and the original decision upheld
- Appeal upheld and the recommended actions
- Appeal partially upheld and no actions or recommended actions.

Not too dissimilar to the disciplinary hearing, the appeal should consider the employee's representations thoroughly. The appeal chair should be looking for evidence to back up any employee assertions and require critical thinking in terms of if there was any wrong doing, procedurally or in the rational for the decision, particularly if these would change the findings of the disciplinary hearing and resulting penalty. In following up from an appeal hearing the letter should confirm the outcome from the appeal, the investigations/research/conversations that were taken in reaching these outcomes and state that the employee has now exhausted their right to appeal on this issue.

In summary, the above outlines the processes that should be followed for employee misconduct – where there is wrong doing – but it does not sit well to take an employee through these processes when there is an intrinsic capability issue i.e. is the misconduct because the employee 'won't do' in which case disciplinary warnings are apt or is the misconduct because the employee 'can't do' due to learning difficulties or mind-set. In the latter the employee has failed to achieve a required level of performance, but crucially has at least tried. In these circumstances, a capability process, where you have formal meetings, not dissimilar to the above outlined disciplinary process should be conducted, but the focus should be on the performance measures and targets.

Performance Management for dismissal.

Normally a first performance meeting will outline and specify clearly the performance problems and the levels of attainment required. The outcome of this first meeting will normally be a performance improvement plan detailing the specifics of the performance required and the timeline for achieving these, with a commitment to review in four, six or eight weeks' time normally. It is good practice to gain the employee's agreement to targets and KPI's in creating the improvement plan. Additionally, where it is practical, cite the organisation's contractual requirements for performance and consequences of not reaching these requirements. Moreover, use examples where previous performance has been satisfactory either by the employee or by a comparator to demonstrate that your performance improvement plan requirements are reasonable.

If the required standards are reasonable but the performance has not improved by the review meeting, then a capability warning might be issued. This warning should outline clear timescales for improvement stating that if there is further failure to attain required standards another warning and ultimately dismissal might follow. Like disciplinary hearings, the employee should be given the right to appeal any capability warning.

Not all organisations have a capability or performance management policy, however, given that capability is one of the fair reasons for dismissal cited in the Employment Rights Act 1996, I would recommend that you consider such a policy for your company.

In summary, dismissals can be complicated and, let's face it, unless you are completely heartless, not something to be relished. However, doing it 'right' in terms of the legal requirements and doing it 'early' can save you time and money further down the road. In my experience, leveraging the short service dismissal route can mean you save a lot of time in future years. It's often best used when you have a problem with an employee that is hard to put your finger on. These issues tend to be attitudinal, for example not fully pulling their weight, 'stirring things' through engaging in office politics and often manifests in tension with other employees resulting in repeated small disputes. These 'issues' can be the hardest to categorise and deal with as they are not specifically misconduct offences or even fully blown performance problems, so many managers put off dealing with them. Instead the employee becomes known as a troublemaker or awkward and managers become apprehensive about invoking formal action for fear that it will lead to a grievance dispute, subtle retribution or even sabotage of work. The best advice I can give if you have a similar problem to this is not to ignore it. Toxic employees affect the whole working environment, and works against an empowerment culture; tolerating subtle bad behaviour makes it ok for all. In these circumstances you need a strong respected manager to continually work with the employee and pull them into line until they conform, are disciplined or resign. If you are uncomfortable about a formal disciplinary or performance route or don't believe the behaviours will be enough for a dismissal, consider reading **Chapter 2: Settlement Agreements** below.

Top tips for dismissing safely.

1. Check the service length of the employee. If it's less than two years you might be able to waive all or some of your procedures, especially if there are no issues relating to protected characteristics and day one rights.
2. Check your contractual obligations – make sure you are not contracted to follow your procedures if employees have less than two years' service.
3. Consider if suspension might be required to protect other employees or service users. Suspension should be almost always be considered if gross misconduct might be concluded; however, be mindful that this in itself could be seen as a prejudgement on the case and not a neutral act.
4. Make sure your disciplinary procedures are robust and have clauses to allow your company to ask employees to come into disciplinary hearings even when they are off sick.
5. If there is a complex disciplinary issue with witnesses, make sure you conduct a thorough investigation and that all questions and angles are answered.
6. Conclude the investigation with findings and reasons for why misconduct is being found in the case, normally relating the allegations for misconduct back to the company's disciplinary procedure list of misconduct-related offences.
7. Ensure that an independent person to the manager (if they are involved), or any witnesses or the investigators, hear the disciplinary.
8. Make sure you take copies of all paperwork sent to the employee and keep emails, both printed and soft copies in the employee's file. Ideally give disciplinary letter invitations and investigation notes by hand or email, failing that send them recorded or special delivery and also send a second copy through the normal post.

9. Back up any minor misconduct offences with 'letters of concern' (informal warnings) or emails to reiterate why the misconduct was unsatisfactory and that it could lead to further disciplinary sanctions.
10. If you're thinking of dismissing an employee make sure that is stated in the invite letter.
11. In outcome letters for warnings or dismissals ensure you always give the right of appeal. Make sure the appeal manager is somebody impartial and somebody who hasn't been involved in the previous disciplinary hearing or investigation.
12. Make sure that the reasons listed for dismissal were those that you covered in the disciplinary hearing.
13. If you feel you cannot dismiss safely because there are too many risks take the option to consider a settlement agreement. This agreement is explored in the following chapter. This is a way of ensuring that the employee does not subsequently go to an employment tribunal.

□

2

SETTLEMENT AGREEMENTS: THE SECRET WEAPON TO PROTECTING YOUR BUSINESS

The introduction of settlement agreements.

EVER heard about people being given a black plastic bag and asked to clear their desks, leaving their employment in hours? Ever wondered how the big firms managed to get away with it? Well, they did it under a tightly written agreement now known as 'Settlement Agreements', but formerly known as 'Compromise Agreements', where the leaver was paid large sums of money as compensation. It was generally used in the 'City' of London to remove people from senior positions.

In 2014, the government introduced legislation to allow settlement agreements to become statute law. This means an employer can now leverage a settlement agreement to terminate an employment relationship with a one-off payment to an employee, legally, without having to follow the usual dismissal routes available to them.

What value can they offer my business?

There are several benefits of using settlement agreements. You can:

- minimise disparagement against your business,
- include confidentiality clauses to incentivise confidentiality on processes and data held in your business,
- but most importantly you are closing down the option for the employee to take you to an employment tribunal at a later date. In a well-worded settlement agreement an employee

writes off all of their employment rights and forfeits their ability to make a claim at an employment tribunal. It is of course key to make sure that the settlement agreement does cover all the angles.

As a business owner you should consider the strategic value of settlement agreements. Is it the right thing for your business to leverage this kind of termination? Consider how the use will affect your culture. Settlement agreements should definitely not replace good management practices as they can be costly to your business and may make other employees feel unsettled, worrying that they might be next. Equally though, there is often a time and a place for a settlement agreement to be leveraged – for instance, where a dispute is ongoing, lengthy and complicated, and a normal dismissal has considerable risk associated with it.

You might decide that a settlement agreement is the right thing for you and your business and you can use one in many scenarios:

- Where you might have a dispute about performance.
- Where somebody's just not doing their job and talking to them hasn't helped.
- Where an individual no longer wants to be with the organisation and is just going through the motions of work – this is not healthy for the business.
- Where there has been a long history of absence that is disability-related or where the member of staff may be covered by the Equality Act.

What is covered in a settlement agreement?

A well-written settlement agreement should provision for all the potential statute claims, discrimination claims in the Equality Act, unfair dismissal claims, unlawful deductions of wage claims and also breach of contract claims. Another protection, to look out for, or to insist upon if your lawyer is drafting a settlement agreement for you, is to close down any potential for injury claims that may be hanging in the air when the agreement is being drafted, or indeed any future claims an employee may think about bringing. If an employee later tries to start action against you for any injury, you would be able counter-sue them for those payments made as part of the settlement back for breach of the agreement.

Sounds too good to be true? Well there are two catches:

1. Obviously you have to pay the employee and it has to be the right sum of money to incentivise the proceedings.
2. The employee needs to go to a solicitor. To make this type of agreement solid and sound, it has to be signed off by an independent legal adviser that the employee has consulted. The advisor is obliged to show them the agreement that has been drafted on their behalf and to explain what it means in layman's terms, including clarifying what rights they are waiving by signing it. This means that the agreement can be upheld legally, but it is often the case that the employer is expected to pay a reasonable sum of money for the employee to go and speak to an adviser. The adviser could be a Citizen's Advice representative, but more normally is a solicitor who would be expected to declare that they have a practising certificate from the Law Society of England or Scotland. There is an appendix or schedule in the settlement agreement that the adviser signs to declare that they have provided the independent advice and are qualified to do so.

ACAS provides many templates for settlement agreements that you can use. They tend to be fairly basic and don't necessarily cover all the aspects we've talked about above, but you can certainly use them as a good starter – particularly helpful is their offer letter for a settlement agreement.

What is the process?

Prior to issuing an offer letter for a settlement agreement, the first important step is to have a conversation with the employee. How do I suggest you handle that? In my experience, the best way to approach a settlement, as a course of action, is to make it clear to the employee that it is only one of a number of options available to them and is not an ultimatum. Which, happily, is how the legislation is set up in some respects. There is a ten-day period for the employee to contemplate the offer you've made them, which should be in writing, and if your offer is appealing enough, they may prefer to take the offer rather than going through the motions in a role that makes them unhappy or uncomfortable. The alternative option should be spelt out to the employee that they can stay with the business knowing that there are proposed changes on the horizon. It is worth always detailing everything to the employee in the initial conversations to effectively manage the expectations. For example, if you're going to introduce a more comprehensive absence policy and you're concerned that an employee is going to fall foul of the new measures fairly immediately because of their absence record, it might be worth explaining ('explaining' is discussed below) to them that there is an option to 'take some money and run' by means of a settlement versus enduring the new regime. This option might be considered as being fair to both employee and employer as the action is a lot more straightforward than, say, a series of comprehensive and painful absence management meetings with the inevitable result of a dismissal for incapability.

In planning the settlement conversation, I suggest that you have somebody with you in the meeting who you trust and who is a calming influence. Spend some time with this person beforehand, scoping out how the conversation might run, what the employee's reactions are likely to be, and what language you feel is appropriate in this situation. Language, tone and even body language are key. Start by outlining the company's position factually, and without judgement, ideally removing anything that could be construed as personal. Show very clearly the issue that the business is faced with, which might be that the skill set requirements have moved beyond the employee's capacity and/or capabilities, or it might be that the department is losing money and redundancies are the alternative. State the issue succinctly and sensitively, without sounding like an accusation or appointing blame. Questioning the employee about their current happiness and satisfaction in their role and in the business can often make it an easier conversation, particularly if the employee concedes they are not happy or admits to not feeling able to do their job.

Do not make any assumptions about how the employee feels – allow them to open up to you and try to be sympathetic. If there are things they want to get off their chest then listen. It's a great opportunity to gauge the current atmosphere of your business. Where the employee actually agrees with some of the summary statements that you've made, but stops short of admitting any responsibility for the issues, that may be a point where you suggest that you would like the employee to consider if they really want to be with the business given the complaints that they've had of late. For example, "We accept that you and your manager, Lindsey, have not been seeing eye-to-eye, however, it is unlikely that Lindsey will change her requirements and management style for you specifically, therefore you may wish to consider if you can continue to work here." You then outline the performance improvements you will be requiring and any monitoring that will be undertaken.

Then carrying on the conversation with the employee, "Alternatively, if working with Lindsey and making the outlined changes are actions you'd prefer not to take, we could move this conversation on to discussing coming to an arrangement where you exit the business for a small sum of money…" If the employee seems amenable to that discussion, then there are a few things that you, the employer, should know and be aware of, about the conversation you're about to have.

Off-the-record conversations.

It is permissible under law, to have an off-the-record conversation with the employee. Because it is off-the-record, it is a chance for both parties to have a frank and open discussion – indeed, if anybody has been taking notes up until this point you should make clear that notes will not be taken and pens are to be put down. This helps to set scene and provides a visual clue to reinforce the off-the-record nature of the talk.

So here's a brief introduction to the two main types of possible conversation you can have with the employee:

a) Without prejudice conversations
b) Protected conversations

Both types of conversation are off-the-record, which means they cannot normally be referenced at a tribunal. However the big difference between the two is that a conversation on a 'without prejudice' basis should only be used if there is an existing dispute between employer and employee and should only take place with a view to settling the dispute. But what if a business wants to dismiss an employee where there is no formal dispute? The answer is 'Protected Conversations' which were introduced in 2013 with 'Settlement Agreements' and afford employers protection from unfair dismissal claims only. A protected conversation can be invoked at any time as long as they take place with a view to establishing a settlement. You need to be aware that the cover of off-the-record protection could be removed with the conversation later referenced at a tribunal to establish whether an employee was in fact more likely to have been dismissed or offered a settlement agreement related to a discriminatory factor. For example, a conversation that went along the lines of:

"Lindsey feels you and her just don't get along and you're not a good fit for the department, most likely because your priorities…

- have changed since your maternity leave."
- are to leave early on a Friday to be home before sunset."
- you are distracted a bit more since the diagnosis."

"So we'd like to propose a settlement option to you."

Clearly from this example, there are a number of matters relating to holding an off-the-record conversation that are too detailed to go into within this text, and so you may wish to take advice on how you manage these sensitive conversations. Solve HR can offer advice in this area. However, a basic structure to an 'off the record conversation' would be in the following format:

- You should begin the discussion by raising the issue and the likely next steps. You might explain that the issue places him/her at risk of redundancy and clarify the Company's position that the next steps could be performance management, or a disciplinary hearing (whichever is appropriate). It could also mean an outstanding grievance against another employee or member of management.
- Only after you have you discussed this, taking care to outline the seriousness of the situation, and the options available to employee and company through legitimate routes can you then suggest the possibility of entering into a confidential pre-termination discussion – at this point check that he/she agrees to such a discussion. Highlight that you wish to table a pragmatic option to solving a problem and that you need their understanding and agreement that what you are about to propose is on a without prejudice or protected discussion basis.
- Take the opportunity to suggest the option of a settlement agreement where you would pay him/her an agreed sum in return for him/her leaving the Company. This agreement would also prohibit him/her from bringing any claims against the Company in an employment tribunal.
- Explain that any agreement would have to be approved by an advisor, which is normally a solicitor and that the company

will pay a contribution towards this cost for him/her to seek this advice. Make it clear also that this is the most the company will contribute to independent advice if he/she agrees to this path.

- Doing this after you have discussed the above issues will allow him/her to consider his/her position, in the light of his/her conduct, capabilities and potential redundancy.
- Naturally, in most situations, he/she will want to know how much money is involved. If you have avoided writing to the employee in advance and this is an early conversation, it may not be the right thing to do to have figures ready, because it may infer that the decision is a 'fait accompli'. Say that you will go away and consider a fair offer.
- During such discussions, avoid putting too much pressure on him/her – give him/her time to consider his/her position and give you an answer as to whether or not this is a route which he/she would like to go down. ACAS recommend that you provide him/her with a minimum of 10 calendar days to consider your offer although this can be reduced by mutual agreement by both parties. Make it clear you will give the employee time to think it over and discuss with his/her family.
- Explain to the employee that you are about to suggest a deadline that balances the employee's time to think over your proposal and your requirements to know where you stand. Be aware, that this is not always the right course of action, particularly if the employee has been unwell. If you think it appropriate, arrange another meeting with him/her in 10 days' time (or suggest the employee lets you know if he/she has reached a decision before the end of the 10 days). Giving the employee adequate time to consider his/her position decreases the chance of a further dispute or trip to a tribunal and ensures you comply with the code of practice.
- If it is appropriate to go into the financials, I advise that you outline the figures and make clear what is subject to tax and national insurance deductions. These figures include:
  a) Any redundancy and/or ex-gratia payment; these are tax free only up to £30,000.
  b) A notice payment.
  c) Accrued and untaken holiday pay (if relevant) (subject to Tax and National insurance).

d) Any payment for the return of company shares – please seek advice on this.
e) Any payment for benefits such as pension or car allowance or any proposal for benefits to run on longer than the termination agreement.
f) The contribution towards his/her legal fees.

- You may wish to offer him/her a few days of paid leave to consider your offer, however, you are under no obligation to do so.

After the conversation, the process itself is quite simple: if the employee has indicated they'd be interested in reviewing an offer, issue them with a letter. Again ACAS is a good source for the basic letter template, available from their website, and it will give you certain wording that you potentially should have in that letter. The letter should outline, that a 'Protected Conversation' or discussion on a 'Without-prejudice' basis has taken place around the subject of terminating employment; what payments they are eligible for, including payments related to any outstanding holiday accrued and any pay in lieu of notice; and a proposed deadline date for the employee to make their decision - which should be no shorter than ten working days. I would suggest you also put in a time limit/ deadline on how long the offer is open for and also how long you might hold the option to leave with a payment open even if they initially decline but later were to change their mind.

For example:
"In consideration of this offer, we require an indication of your intentions by 5:00pm on the 30th September. You may change your mind after this date for a further month, however, we are unable to guarantee beyond the 30th September that the same package will be on offer."

The final paragraphs of the letter should include the requirement for the employee to go to an independent adviser to sign off the settlement arrangement. This ensures that they get advice and an interpretation on what the legal clauses in the settlement agreement mean so they understand fully the implications and obligations of agreeing to it. It is normal practice for the employer to pay for the employee's costs of legal advice. However, through experience I would encourage you to outline in the letter what amount you are willing to pay towards the cost of their independent adviser. State clearly, that this is a capped contribution beyond which your business will not pay, and let them know what amount that cap is, given market rates. This prevents your business having to pay out more in the event their nominated solicitor attempts to renegotiate their fee. If the solicitor does seek to renegotiate the fee, unless it is a particularly complex termination or agreement where an increase is justified, just decline and if you're explicit with the employee in the offer letter then the chances of solicitors requesting more money in first place will be dramatically reduced.

Where your solicitor or in-house HR manager has created and proofed the agreement, a reasonable fee is normally between £300 to £450+VAT, depending on what region of the UK you are in. When settlement agreements are relatively straightforward employment solicitors will not normally have to spend many hours on reviewing the agreement, talking with the employee and signing it off.

On the other hand, where the situation becomes a little more complicated with the solicitor coming back with reasonable demands for their client, or you find that your position in the negotiations is getting weaker, or that changes to the agreement are warranted, then it's your call whether you cover the increased costs or not. However, if the agreement is written well in the first place, understanding and closing down most potential risks, it's very unlikely that the employee's solicitor will have to do much work and therefore cannot reasonably justify higher costs. It is generally viewed as a tick-box exercise for many solicitors and employees alike, and as an employee is able to go to a Citizen's Advice adviser and receive this support for free I suggest that the cost-per-hour that some solicitors charge for this service is not warranted – though I'm sure many will argue differently, of course!

If the employee accepts the offer letter you need to agree with the employee what their termination date will be, and you may come to a compromise on this date. As mentioned previously, you will be required to pay the employee for any outstanding accrued holidays and benefits up to the termination date. Also, don't forget about any loans or training costs that the business may have paid to or on behalf of the employee. These can all be offset against any final termination payments, if your settlement agreement outlines this and you choose to implement this. Once agreed and signed, remember to check what the agreement says in terms of your obligations for making the settlement payment and ensure in the first instance that the agreement stipulates payment is only due on receipt of 'a properly signed agreement and supporting documents.' Settlement payments often can't be due ten days after receipt of the agreement so don't assume that you can just schedule the payment for the next payroll run. Once it has been signed by all parties, (i.e. you, the employee and the independent solicitor), keep the agreement on file.

Top tips on Settlement Agreements.

1. Leverage the ACAS documentation and guidance for straightforward settlement agreement dismissals, if appropriate.
2. Always have difficult conversations on both a 'without prejudice' and 'protected conversation' basis, particularly where there are potential discrimination claims.
3. Present the choices to the employee and spell out the options. Take care to ensure it is not presented as a fait accompli.

Be clear with the employee on how much you will contribute towards their independent lawyer/solicitor and ask the employee to be clear with their chosen advisor that that is the available budget and you will not negotiate an increase.

3

BUYING A BUSINESS AND THE EMPLOYEES THAT GO WITH THEM

WHEN you're looking at buying a business or a franchise that already exists you have to consider what is known in employment law as 'TUPE'. TUPE stands for: Transfer of Undertakings Protection of Employment legislation. If the business is a 'going concern' when purchased, on most occasions, all of the existing employees transfer to the new owners of that business. This is quite common in the service industry, for example: cafés, cleaning companies, printers and transport. If you're considering buying a franchise, a café, or a cleaning business, you need to think about more than just the purchase price of the business. A good lawyer will always instruct you to do 'due diligence' and find out as much as you possibly can that will help to determine the true value of the business and any liabilities involved in taking it over. This will help in any negotiations – remember you don't need to accept the price they've asked.

Oftentimes, because of the cost of a lawyer, people are reluctant to seek advice and prefer to gather information in a more informal way, such as having a friendly discussion with the owner. However, this may not yield all the information required in order to confidently put a value on that business; before agreeing to any purchase price, make sure that you know exactly what responsibilities you will inherit. One of the most important questions to ask about existing staff is do they have contracts of employment? Ask to see the contracts if they do. Otherwise, you could potentially be taking on a great deal of risk, unusual obligations, an unsustainable pay scheme, and the only way to avoid adverse factors like these is to have all the data upfront. I encourage you to be methodical and appreciate that the human assets of the business, the employees, are used to a particular way of working, they already have expectations of how they ought to be treated and they may even have plans that depend on the current status quo of the business, for example they might have holidays lined up.

Things to ask before you buy:

- Does the business have contracts of employment? If so, is there a restrictive covenant in the Contract or alongside the contract?
- How do the day to day practices differ from the contracts of employment?
- If so, are they up-to-date?
- Do all members of staff have a contract?
- Does the contract state hours of work?
- Does it state the hourly remuneration rate?
- What is the sickness policy? And who is presently off sick, including long-term illness?
- What is the holiday policy? And who has leave planned?
- What benefits are provided to employees?
- What else is covered in the contract?
- What financial records are there?
- What customer information is there?
- What pension scheme is in place? Is it compliant with the Pensions Act?
- Who are the suppliers and what are their details?

I've worked with many small businesses owners who have bought a café, a hairdressing salon or equivalent, with the best of intentions, then found the previous owner practices that were not completely legitimate e.g. undeclared cash-in-hand payments. I can understand why some business owners choose to do that, but if an employee is regularly getting a top-up of a £500 a month cash-in-hand, and you wanted to change to legitimately putting it through the books, then as they will now have to pay tax on it, their net income will reduce and this could affect your relationship (though not with the taxman!). Word to the wise: remember how custom and practice works. For a reminder see the first section of **Chapter 1: Dismissing Safely.**

So be very careful about getting your data, but more importantly, ensure that your lawyer allows protective warranties in the purchase of a business in the event that you subsequently find that the disclosure of information was not as complete or true to what you were led to believe.

Often if an employee was on long-term sick you would have to transfer them across the same as every other employee; even if they're not getting paid for being off on long-term sick, you are likely to inherit the obligation to manage them in the business, get them back to work (which could be costly), or, in the event that they don't come back to work, you could be potentially liable for a tribunal claim if you terminate them for ill health. The important thing to note about TUPE is that the liability is joint, so that means that the existing business owners and the new business owners are liable jointly for any resulting tribunal claim. You have to be mindful when you're selling a business too, that you're selling it to somebody who understands and wants to protect their own interests as well as yours someone who is not going to treat employees very poorly and subsequently open you both to being sued at a tribunal.

We have a client who experienced this problem after selling shares in a business. They didn't consult with us in the first instance because believed there was no TUPE requirement because it was 'only a transfer of shares'. The new majority shareholder of the business went on to claim that the Operations Manager role was redundant dismissing the inherited incumbent on that basis, but then filled that role themselves. Clearly, the role therefore was not redundant. Also the new owner did not follow a legal redundancy process for the previous Operations Manager. Although my client, the original shareholder, did not know about the new shareholders' intentions or their actions, the ex-employee claimed a TUPE transfer took place, the client failed to follow their legal TUPE consultation obligations and that made the dismissal unfair.

As I outlined above, the legislation affords for consultation when there's a transfer of a going concern. Both parties, the existing business owner and the new business owner, are obliged to consult with employees. With a small group of employees it's easy to facilitate consultation. If there are normally over ten employees in the business you are obliged to consult collectively but you could ask employees and representatives if they would be happy to consult individually. If they wish individual consultation then it is necessary to have one-to-one meetings with them. If they're happy to be consulted as a group then the employees should appoint an employee representative who will be appraised in meetings with you about the transfer, and who then goes back to their fellow employees and colleagues to disseminate the information they have learnt.

The main points when considering buying a business.

Consultation can be done relatively easily: you have to meet with employees and check their terms and conditions off against the information that you've been given. Normally the requirement is that the business provides the new owners with all the employee data twenty-eight days in advance of any transfer date. Sometimes this is pretty difficult to achieve for a number of reasons. One factor may be that people in business tend to play their cards close to their chest and protect their data until after the apparent liability has been safely passed on. This detailed list of information is quite comprehensive. It includes employees' names, addresses, dates of birth, their salaries, etc. Some of the data can be anonymised prior to the purchase date, and in fact prior to the due diligence stage, but when it gets close to a transfer, all the data, the contracts of employment and the templates need to be transferred over to the new incumbent within the statutory rules. The new owner on Day One, or even before, should be consulting with their newly-inherited staff. You're legally allowed to go into the transferring business and have meetings with staff to give presentations about the transition process, or about the business doing the acquiring, to reassure employees and make them aware of what they can expect, and introduce any new measures that the buyers of the business are planning.

Anything that may affect the employees transferring in terms of their contract of employment ought to be disclosed and there is a requirement from both transferor and transferee to put in writing to the staff (both pre- and post-transfer) the intentions, transfer dates and an acknowledgement that the existing contract of employment will be honoured. Any redundancies and/or proposed changes to terms and conditions of employment have to be disclosed and it has to be clear that these changes or proposed redundancies are not purely to facilitate an easy transfer. If an employee feels they have been adversely affected by changes brought in as part of the transfer, you could end up with a tribunal on your hands. So you probably need to seek quite comprehensive advice on TUPE if you have changes planned. Don't find yourself in a situation where an employee is coming at you with an unfair dismissal claim and they're also claiming that you've breached the TUPE regulations and guidelines. Normally changes can be made to existing contracts of employment, but only in certain circumstances which the legislation cites for reasons such as economic, technological or organisational. However, it's definitely worth getting advice before making changes as the case law and the statute for this are quite complex.

If you find yourself inheriting a group of employees where their contracts of employment are pretty simple – there's maybe a minimum hours or zero hours contract established and therefore there appears not to be any enhanced obligations – then make sure that you capture from the outgoing employer the actual working hours that employees have been doing for the twelve weeks previous. This will give you an indication of what implicit contractual obligations you may have to these employees. Just because a contact states 'zero hours' does not mean that this cannot be overwritten by custom and practice as we discussed in **Chapter 1: Dismissing Safely.** You may end up having an obligation to give your new employees forty hours per week regardless of their contract of employment, because this is what they have been working for years. Just to reiterate, get a clear indication from the outgoing employer of the pattern of work for the last twelve weeks – ideally more – of the working hours in practice. If it's a seasonal type of business, like hospitality, where the hours of work fluctuate greatly between summer months and winter months, to get the best information on this situation, ask for a twelve-month calendar year of working hours for the employees in existence. You can then work out their average hours per week or your average cost obligations to them.

One of the most important points in data collection is establishing employees' lengths of service, understanding how many long serving employees you are inheriting, and what your obligations might be to them. Why? Because if you are considering reducing the workload or if you're buying into a business and your existing business already performs the same or similar functions, you may end up having too many people in a similar position and therefore need to downsize in the future. In this event, you may decide to 'pool' the individuals in your present business with those from the new business to work out who stays and who goes as part of a redundancy process. Their years of service for the old business and their age will impact on the cost of their redundancy and thus your overall merger/acquisition costs.

So, there's a lot of complicated thought around purchasing a business. Sometimes when it appears quite straightforward, there are still pitfalls. My philosophy is "forewarned is forearmed". It's worth looking also at what restrictive covenants and confidential clauses the current/selling owners have in place for protecting the business IP or client list; after all the idea of paying for a business is to purchase the goodwill clients and processes the business has established over the years. If, for example you're buying a hairdressing salon and the employed hairdressers have a non-compete agreement in their existing contract of employment and you're bringing their contract of employment across to your ownership under TUPE then you're protected better, as the employees will be still obligated by these non-compete clauses and shouldn't be running off to set up a shop two doors down. If there is a restrictive covenant, ask yourself this: does it give you enough cover in the event that the top talent decides to resign three months after you buy the business?

Also, what protections do you have against the outgoing owner starting up again and stealing clients or intellectual property? These are things that you want to check in your due diligence, to ensure that your business or new investment is protected adequately.

Top tips for buying a business:

1. Do your research, ask questions and get the details.
2. If possible try and meet with all the employees or at least some before you sign on the dotted line and ask questions about their terms and conditions.
3. Remember if you are inheriting employers you have an obligation to consult with your new employees as does the 'selling' employer.
4. Remember you will become liable for the actions of the outgoing employer – don't land yourself with an employment tribunal before you've already started! Cover yourself in the commercial agreement and allow a contingency for this.
5. Listen to your 'gut'. If you think the seller is withholding something or not being honest, ask for the evidence to

support or rule out your suspicions.

6. Do your sums and ensure you have a firm grasp of the total staff costs. Use the 1.5 multiple of the basic salary to account for benefits, expenses pension and NI costs.
7. Have an independent and knowledgeable person look at the agreement 'heads of terms' and explain your liabilities.
8. Ensure you receive a 12 month or at least a 12 week rota or log of hours from before the point of transfer, which details each individuals hours of work. Particularly if the contract of employment lists zero or variable hours.

4

MAKING CHANGES AS YOUR BUSINESS CHANGES: GETTING 'FIT FOR PURPOSE' OR DOWNSIZING

Restructuring.

BUSINESSES evolve over time, and their structures often need to change to remain fit for purpose. Making these changes safely should be a priority.

Oftentimes, some changes can be made pretty easily and just speaking to employees and changing factors such as job titles (with their agreement!) can be enough. However, sometimes contentious issues can arise: perhaps an employee doesn't like the new job description or the job title they've been offered and starts to create a fuss. It's worthwhile to look at the changes you want to make from the employee's point of view – putting their shoes on your feet, so to speak – and making sure that when you are changing the business around them, you're continually communicating the reasons why the changes are taking place.

Something that Simon Sinek, author and motivational speaker on leadership practices, strongly advocates, and that I agree with, is that ensuring employees understand the reasons behind any business change is a fundamental contributor to any successful business. This does not mean they have to agree with your decisions, but when they understand the reasoning behind your decisions, there is a greater chance of employee acceptance. I find issues are minimised when communication is maintained.

Whether embarking on a few tweaks to minor processes or restructuring the entire organisation, there is a way to protect your business from ending in a mess of tribunal claims. The rule of thumb is you should handle change to the employees' terms and conditions conscientiously and formally. Ordinarily, everybody joins a business on a contract of employment which specifies their hours of work, their job title, their place of work and other key factors. If any of those terms change fundamentally, particularly a job title or place of work, then a formal approach through a recorded consultation process is needed to make the changes.

Firstly, start with the business case. Creating the business case gives you an opportunity to take a step back and clarify your rationale for the changes. No doubt you're very clear on the reasons for the need to change – you might be able to show through the financials that a department is losing money, or that sales have declined for a certain product. You'll also be clear on the benefits these changes will bring to you and the business – that changes to salaries, hours of work, job titles, locations of work, etc, will save money, improve succession planning for the business, or increase efficiency.

The changes may even result in longer term protection of jobs in that reducing headcount through a restructure with one or two redundancies in the short-term will protect the rest of the workforce's positions in the long-term, then state it. In short, you'll have seen the problem, identified a solution and worked out the benefits of the solution; now formalise that in a documented business case at the earliest stage even before embarking on any consultation or even announcing any proposed changes.

By writing them down you have an informative document to use during consultation briefs but also which can be referenced in any tribunal challenge (especially where an employee is not happy with their change of job or redundancy and believes and/or insinuates that the changes were a sham used specifically to remove them from the business, which some businesses are guilty of doing). Avoid the mistake of not writing down your reasons and you'll be able to help any potential tribunal establish that redundancies and changes were made for legitimate business reasons.

Secondly, now it's time to address the workforce. Business case in hand you can engage in a formal consultation process with all employees. Giving employees the written proposal allows them to examine this for themselves and offers them the opportunity to join the discussion. I believe people are happier with changes when they feel they have been involved in the process and decisions. It's very important to use the right language during the consultation stages, i.e. 'It's a proposal at this stage' until you have consulted thoroughly with all members of staff.

Thirdly, after the consultation is concluded, confirm to the employees the results in writing. Only then can you start to think about actually making the changes.

For example:
Consider an organisation which has three Accounts Assistants doing similar jobs, but the now the Accounts team requires instead a more senior person with a stronger skill set and greater knowledge of the finance systems in use and who has experience managing people. The details will be specific to your business, but in the above hypothetical scenario, the proposed change is the creation of an Accounts Manager role.

New structures and suitable alternatives.
Once the high level business case is agreed and written down the normal practice is to create a 'before and after' visual, namely, what the state of play for the organisation is now, and what it will look like if the proposed actions go ahead. The next step is to consider carefully the new job roles proposed under the new structure. It's really helpful to have an organisation structure chart that's current and that reflects the business now. It's then relatively easy to create an organisational chart that reflects the business in its proposed future state which can be given to managers and employees to help them visualise how the nuts and bolts of the proposal will work. In the Accounts Assistants example the organisation structure (described in what is normally called an 'org chart') would move from 3 Accounts Assistants alongside each other to one Accounts Manager above one Accounts Assistant. Attached to these new organisation charts, I recommend having proposed job descriptions that show the new job titles and their associated tasks and duties, should the proposal be agreed. This can help employees see if their future exists in the new business structure and it also helps you and your managers

evaluate what are called 'suitable alternatives' if needed. A 'suitable alternative' applies where you're changing somebody's present role into a slightly different one in the restructured environment where tasks and duties are similar and the skill sets are comparable. This should encourage them to take the new role as it reduces their risk of being made redundant.

Sometimes, however, the employee does not like the new role. The reasons for this could be endless: fear of change; dislike of a new manager; or as in many cases they have already come around to the idea of leaving and even have plans for how they will spend their redundancy payment. However, in a suitable alternative situation where they are determined not to accept the new post and instead wish to leave there may be an argument that they would not be eligible for a redundancy payment. In this situation, they would have to resign or you would have to write to them to end their current contract of employment and re-engage them on your new terms and conditions, provided of course you have followed the proper consultation process. However, this is not without risk, namely a constructive dismissal claim at the high end of the risk factor and at the low end the risk of keeping on a disengaged, bitter employee who may trudge on unhappily in the new post, and who may consciously or unconsciously sabotage your new structure.

Situations like this make it clear how important job descriptions can be. They can also serve a second purpose in that they can reinstate and clarify the business' aims and objectives as outlined in the business rationale at the department and individual level. Once you have your business rationale, consider: does this new organisational structure and these new job descriptions reflect the new story and the new world that you're anticipating? Does your rationale cover everything? I've experienced some very complicated restructures and I've often seen change managers who, in the midst of working through the consultancy processes with those that were at risk, looked at the job descriptions created and actually decided that other members of staff were able to fill those roles. I've even experienced situations whereby in the initial 'rationale drafting' stages or later through consultation feedback, the change managers identify in the new job descriptions that there are actually too many activities listed and decided to split a role down to two to better serve the organisation's purposes. So, taking the time to look at job descriptions with a blank piece of paper can really help solidify your views of what you are looking to achieve overall, which again in turn helps to protect your business from any tribunal claims in the future.

Announcing change.
Once you have your job descriptions, the next challenge is to appraise and address the teams that will be affected, although eventually some communication should go out to all employees. It's quite important, when carrying out a proper restructure, that you consider who will be affected and who will be unaffected and separate those teams out because they will have to be addressed differently. Following on from the earlier advice on announcement and communication briefing, the brief that you give to the unaffected member of staff is likely to be different to the brief to the affected members of staff. The affected members of staff in a restructure may be getting a message that if the worst comes to the worst, redundancies may be at play here if the new posts cannot be successfully filled, even though it is not necessarily a redundancy exercise. Whereas the unaffected members of staff will likely need strong reassurance that redundancies are not going to befall them. Communicate strongly that they are safe! Equally if you think that you're embarking on a change that might eventually affect the currently unaffected business areas and staff, think about how you temper your message. You want communication to be as transparent and as honest as possible without scaring your employees or rocking the boat unnecessarily; you still have a business to run after all. You don't want to find that in a year's time you're being called out for not giving them the whole truth upfront. That will undermine your integrity and can cause wider deep-rooted mistrust and disengagement. So if you do have a concern about their (the presently unaffected) business unit or you know for a fact that they're next, look at drafting a very eloquent, sympathetic message to capture this. For the affected members of a team, once you have the names of individuals listed, the other information you need to have at hand are their job titles, their start dates, their ages, and any potential redundancy payments you might consider offering them if they were to be made redundant or to decide to leave the business. Here is an example of data collection for redundancy.

Table 1: Example Statutory Redundancy Settlement Entitlements:

Current Structure and those affected example:- PRIVATE & CONFIDENTIAL

Department / Team	Job Title	Name	Date of Birth	Start Date	Monthly Gross	Maximum Statutory Redundancy Entitlement	Notice Period	Notice pay if not working	Qualify for suitable alternative
Marketing	Marketing Associate	Ryan Wishling	04/07/1973	03/04/2012	£2,220 pm	£2,634	6 weeks	£3,073.84	No
Marketing	Marketing Administrator	Toby Ranway	16/08/1980	10/04/2014	£1,500 pm	£1,038	N/A	N/A	Yes. Admininstration assistant or PA.
Marketing	Marketing Manager	Ashley Bingham	10/02/1965	05/01/2017	£3,200 pm	Doesn't qualify as less than 2 years service	2 weeks	£1,476.92	No

In 2018/2019 financial year, weekly pay is capped at £508 per week, with a 1.5x multiple for those aged over 41 years.

If you're not considering redundancies at all - which is actually quite rare in a restructure because a restructure looks at improving efficiency – then having a comprehensive job description that describes changes to the size, nature and remuneration for a particular new role, is essential. For the one remaining Accounts Assistant, in our example, restating what the role includes and excludes would be important as it is the amalgamation of three into one. Likewise, explaining what activities would be picked up by the new Manager would help to explain the skillset required for the more senior post as well as clarifying what activities would no longer be conducted by the more junior staff member. You can then go out into the marketplace and price the roles appropriately and communicate to staff the roles and their salaries in the new structure. Then it becomes clear to them that they may be placed in the new role due to it being classed as a 'suitable alternative' or they might even choose to apply or preference for a new role. It's a good idea to state the salaries for any newly created jobs, as staff can then can then decide if they want to move into them by preferencing or applying for them, opt to take voluntary redundancy (if it's available) or even wait until they are made compulsorily redundant. For our Accounts Assistants a clear view of the skillset required for the Managerial role might make the affected staff realise they would not be considered for that role, in which case there could be two redundancies from three staff.

In many circumstances where redundancies aren't on the table you may not need to go as far as completing a full restructure process and could potentially make desired changes through initial conversations and first formal consultations. However, you will have to have more formal consultation meetings if you're looking to change contractual terms and conditions (salary, hours of work, location of work, benefits). After formally consulting with staff and clarifying that there are no redundancies but that there is a compelling business case for changing the main terms and conditions, if you find you cannot reach an agreement with a group or even one or two individuals, the option open to you is to give them notice that you are going to terminate their existing terms and conditions/contract of employment. You have to dismiss them and then invite them to be re-engaged on the new terms and conditions. Of course this is not without risk but it's an option to be considered. The risk in question is a claim of unfair dismissal and breach of contract and perhaps other claims that a solicitor may attempt to tack on. Hence why you must conduct a proper consultation process and have a crystal clear business case and make sure any selection process is transparent and fair.

Timelines for communications and consultations.

So once you have your teams split up into your unaffected and your affected groups; you've got all the figures and job descriptions for the new structure and the old structure as a comparison. The next thing to do is to create a timetable for all the activities that will take place during the consultation period. Project plan from the day that you will first announce proposed changes to the whole company and address teams; set locations for the consultation meetings and plan what you're going to do immediately afterward. Pay particular attention to the how and when communication will occur. For example, normally I would recommend having a brief informal one-to-one immediately after the announcement with those who will be affected in the changes.

The initial announcement has to make it clear that you are entering a consultation period; it has to be clear how long the company anticipates consulting with staff during this period and if jobs are at risk. Normally a 'meaningful consultation period' for a company with fewer than thirty employees (or thirty members within a business unit to be reorganised), has to be at least between ten and twenty days, as determined by case law. Anything shorter than that and you could be accused of failing to consult properly with the implication that the redundancies were therefore a fait accompli.

There is certain legislation on information and consultation which pertains to redundancies in particular. This states how long a consultation period should be for employers that have over thirty employees that need to be reorganised – normally a thirty-day minimum period. For employers with more than that there are further requirements. Additionally, if you are looking at making around twenty or more redundancies in any ninety-day period, there is a legal requirement to inform the Department for Business, Energy and Industrial Strategy (BEIS) of your intentions to make those redundancies. The BEIS is a merger between the Department for Business, Innovation and Skills (BIS) and the Department of Energy and Climate Change (DECC) and occurred in July 2016.

Failure to follow this requirement can also mean that you fail in your proper obligations on redundancy. Local government must be alerted when there is, what they consider, a significant number of redundancies and thus you need to be careful when identifying your affected employee groupings and consider how long your overall business changes may take and then the number of casualties there realistically will be. Affected employees must receive a written confirmation of their 'at risk' status. The content of the letter should reconfirm all of the points made in the announcement, possibly in slightly briefer terms and should also normally extend an invitation to a first formal consultation where employees will be given the legal right to be accompanied by a companion (another employee from the business) or an accredited trade union representative.

That meeting should take place no earlier than 48 hours of them receiving the letter. However, it should normally be scheduled quite soon after the announcement. I suggest if you make an announcement on a Monday that you aim to have your first formal consultation meeting on the Thursday of that week. That letter is most easily, and I would suggest, most sympathetically, delivered by hand, in the informal consultation session which immediately follows the initial announcement. Ideally this session should be handled by the manager or the announcing manager, along with a verbal personalised explanation of the contents of the letter.

Preferencing and restructuring jobs.

If you are conducting a restructure where there's various different roles being created, you might invite employees to review the job descriptions in the informal session and include the job descriptions in the invitation to the first formal consultation, allowing them to start thinking about the practicalities of the roles proposed and to consider what role they might be interested in. Be careful to reiterate 'in the event these roles are confirmed post-consultation'. If it is a restructure in your letter, ask the employee to come back to you or a point of contact by a certain deadline with their preference of role in the event that the restructure goes ahead. This will allow you to get an indication of how many employees are likely to move into the new structure and what roles they may be comfortable in.

The benefit of having this knowledge in the midst of consultation rather than later is that you're enabling employees to exert some control over the process and their 'destiny'. They might initially be surprised to hear about the changes you propose, shocked or even scared about what will happen to them and their jobs. But by allowing employees to state a preference early on for any of the roles that will be available in the proposed new structure and by allowing them to articulate in this process their potential career aspirations with the company, they can feel more in control of the process and this may alleviate some of their concerns.

Take a situation where you have a new role of 'Finance Manager' and an employee currently in a managerial administration position has applied for this newly–created post although they do not work in the finance department at present. Through the preferencing exercise they state that they have financial qualifications or relevant previous experience; you might then become more open-minded to them moving into that new role, if they were successful in the selection process.

So preferencing is a good exercise for allowing employees to take more control. It can get them to think about the proposed structure in a different way i.e. as an opportunity for them, rather than the end of their road; it shows that you value their views as an essential part of the process and it allows you to see who is committed to a career in the business, it can even reveal skill sets you did not know you possessed or had forgotten about.

Furthermore, you might consider, offering 'discretionary voluntary redundancy', where you ask employees to volunteer for redundancy, setting a deadline date by which they should respond. This can be incentivised by enhancing the redundancy payment from the statutory entitlement, which is capped at £508 per week up to a maximum of £15,240 for redundancies after 6 April 2018. See the www.gov.uk website for details. Years ago, though, many people with long service used to covet redundancy for early retirement as larger employers would offer very generous discretionary redundancy payments schemes often linked to the equivalent of monthly pay for every year of service rather than the statutory method in place today. Nowadays, those large payments are uncommon and you don't need to offer as much as that. Find the balance that works for you though obviously the more you offer the more likely employees are to take you up on the offer.

Making straight forward redundancies: compulsory redundancies.

The above section covers redundancies as an outcome of restructuring roles and jobs in the business to make it more fit for the future or a reduction in the jobs required. However it is often the case that redundancies are a result of a more straightforward business objective, closing an unprofitable department for example or even the complete closure of your business.

The legislation, Employment Rights Act 1996, defines a fair dismissal related to redundancy as:

'an employee is dismissed by reason of redundancy if the dismissal is wholly or mainly attributable to the fact that the employer ceases to carry on the business in which the employee was employed, or cease to carry on that business in the place where the employee was employed. A redundancy will also occur when the needs of the business for the employees to carry out work of a particular kind have ceased or diminished.'

In the first two cases, ordinarily you will not need to define a pool of employees who would be at risk of redundancy as it should be obvious. For example, the body shop of a car dealer in a certain location is closing, or a complete chain of shops is closing due to losses. In these more obvious situations the redundancy process is straightforward.

You need to do the following:

- Create your business rationale- losses to date, sales forecast, increased supplier costs, value of lost commercial contracts, and changes in the economy or customer behaviour.
- The steps you have taken to mitigate loss of jobs- freeze on recruitment, letting temps go, increased sales and marketing drive, collaboration with other businesses.

- Cost out the redundancies, see page 36 for a template on supporting you with this.
- Create an announcement for employees which captures points A and B.
- Plan the process and cater for collective and individual consultation, which is dependent on the number of jobs at risk. A minimum of 30 days for 20 or more redundancies
- Notify the government, the Redundancy Payments Service (RPS) before collective redundancy starts – this is normally 30 days before the confirmation of the first redundancy dismissal, if 20 or more jobs are at risk within a 90 day period. You do this by completing a HR1 form and this can be done online. If more than 100 redundancies are proposed then 45 days is the minimum consultation period aligned to the notice that must be given to the RPS. You can do this by going to https://www.gov.uk/government/publications/redundancy-payments-form-hr1-advance-notification-of-redundancies (correct as at December 2018).
- Create a timetable and schedule in meetings, the scripting of meetings and the briefing of managers and employees or their representatives. Remember that individual consultation requires a letter inviting employees to their consultation meeting (48 hours in advance of the meeting) that should inform them of their right to be accompanied at the meeting. Include in the letter any election of employees' representatives where collective consultation is required. If you have a date of proposed closure, it might be worth working backwards from that date to ensure you comply with the legal timeframes. See the process flow on: https://www.solvehr.co.uk/no_employment_lawyer_required/
- Where a closure is due to the location or increased costs of basing a business in a certain place, you need to make sure that redundancy is in fact the correct option and that staff should not be offered to continue their existing jobs at a different site. Making redundancies is never easy. However, it might be the right thing to preserve jobs elsewhere or protect your livelihood longer term. Whatever the impetus in terms of preparing yourself for redundancies I can offer the following advice:
- Although it will be hard for you, remember it is potentially harder for those being made redundant – they are faced with

uncertainty and immediate change. In short, don't say, 'this is awful for me'. Make it about those at risk and how you will do your best to support them despite the news and their potential redundancy.

- Try and separate yourself from the personal relationships and the business needs. Often this is the hardest thing to do because you will know the people affected, their family, loyalty and skills. However, if you carry this into a restricting or redundancy process you may make fundamental mistakes in terms of dismissing the wrong people or worse keeping people who are too costly.
- Don't consider it a personal failure. Some of the strongest entrepreneurs and leaders have had to make redundancies and down size for various reasons. Resolve to learn from the mistakes you may have made and aspire to be in a stronger positon in the future.

Good luck if you are embarking on a redundancy programme. Make sure you plan thoroughly and communicate with employees throughout to protect any allegations of unfair redundancy dismissals.

When is it ok to recruit for a position that was made redundant?
The short answer to this is around six months. Presently, the claim window for unfair dismissal on the ground of redundancy is open for six months from the date of dismissal. That does not mean you can't recruit at all nor can you recruit for that department, however, I would encourage caution on the job description and the advert you create for any vacancies. We are aware of a case where an ex-employee stumbled across a job advert which all to clearly stated along with other duties the main activities she had been carrying out in a supposedly 'redundant' position. Even though the process had been legitimate and business case at the time robust and the employee paid her redundancy pay the company had got caught out as the individual identified this as her role with some 'extras' bundled in. She raised a claim on the basis the redundancy had been a sham and a way to remove her from her role. The company settled through ACAS conciliation. The lesson here is be very careful if you are going to embark on recruitment not long after redundancies and consider adverts, job descriptions and process carefully.

Top tips for restructuring:

1. To get it right, listen to you customers, employees or review what your business goals are objectives and how close the business is to achieving these against the gaps.
2. Take a blank sheet of paper and imagine if you were starting out fresh and what roles and locations would be optimum for your business.
3. Take people and personalities out of the picture; use job titles and job descriptions and imagine everyone is Joe blogs, your top performer, in each role.
4. Think out of the box, don't rely on traditional work practices. How could IT help? Does everyone need to be in one location?
5. Ensure you spend time on your business case and justifications.
6. Top tips for managing redundancies.
7. Don't forget to consult with your employees.
8. Plan the costs and timescales.
9. Really listen in employee meetings and make sure your pivot and explore ideas and proposals to ensure meaningful consultation.
10. Ask for volunteers.
11. Consider all options and suitable alternative options.
12. Remember this is not about you, and to put the employee who could be out of a job at the forefront on your mind.
13. Consider if settlement agreements have a place in your process.

5

MANAGING SICKNESS AND ABSENCE

Strategies for reducing absence levels.

MANAGING absence can be most employers' major headache, and although it can be complicated, it doesn't need to be complicated. The first and most important thing to have for absence is a thorough and strong absence policy which clearly sets out the employee's obligations in the event that they are ill, or for other types of absences. The Solve HR website holds a free checklist for assessing your absence policy. This is outlined in the short-term absence management section later in this chapter. In addition there are some other practical measures you can consider outlined below:

- Induction.
- Minimising company sick pay.
- Maintaining regular contact.

Induction.

Each employee should receive a comprehensive induction on Day One, ideally from their line manager. A component of that induction should be the absence policy which makes it clear what will happen in the event of short- or long-term absence and the company's expectations of employees over those times. A free checklist of a standard induction process is available on the Solve HR website.

Minimising Company Sick Pay.

Every employee is entitled to Statutory Sick Pay (SSP) provided they qualify for it, and they need to have been off work sick for 4 or more days in a row, including non-working days. At the time of writing SSP is £92.05 for 2018/2019 (up from £89.35 in 2017/2018) per week for up to 28 weeks, payable by the employer. For the latest info see www.gov.uk/statutory-sick-pay.

Statutory requirements aside, a company can create their own sick pay scheme to extend and enhance the statutory limits. However, one of the major deterrents to absence I've seen is not paying for absence, and I always encourage small- and medium-scale enterprises (SMEs) to think about this option when defining their terms and conditions of employment. It can seem harsh and it may not fit with your corporate culture but you will want to balance the harshness and lack of fit with the potential cost that employee absence may present to your business. As a minimum, I would advocate this policy for at least the duration of the probationary period. Ideally though, I would suggest not paying for absence in the first year of employment and only to increase payment for sickness-related absence as time-in-service increases – this is an effective sick pay policy. Another frequently-used option is to leave company sick pay to the discretion of directors, although the potential pitfall of this option is their inconsistent application of discretion. I have worked with companies where Directors in the SME wish to apply their discretion in a certain set of circumstances, such as the employee undergoing an operation or reporting to be suffering from a severe illness like cancer, for example. The Director then agrees upfront with the employee that they will be paid for a certain time period, usually one to three months.

My final note on this matter is that when you are considering a sick pay scheme, in my experience it is much easier to add to a scheme than to take away from it. However, if you do have a sick pay scheme in place and you feel that it is being abused, or rather you don't have a scheme but you still have an absence problem then consider the other management initiatives in the form of an absence policy which are discussed later.

In summary, if you wish to offer a sick pay scheme consider the following options:

- Offering Statutory Sick Pay only, with the ability to exercise manager or director discretion on this payment policy.

- Eligibility for company sick pay at a year or more of service.
- A short amount of days paid for in a 12-month period. For example, five days of company sick pay in a rolling 12-month period. Remember though: five days is a full week and some may consider it to be used like holidays.
- Company Sick Pay increasing with service. A week for every year of service up to four weeks service and thereafter offering eight weeks pay in any rolling 12 month period.

Taking over a business or redrafting contracts? Then check that the new sick pay policy states that any paid company sick pay is in a rolling 12-month calendar period.

For example:
if the first day of sickness was 1st of April and you afford one weeks' pay/five days and they are off for a week, then they don't qualify for sick pay again until the 6th of April the following year. Very often the terms of the contract or the handbook policy are not clear enough, which opens the door to an employee being absent for 4-6 months, returning for a week (which restarts their company sick pay entitlement) and then going off again. In which case they're paid continuously for absence! If this is in the contract of employment there is very little an employer can do. Having it on a 12-month basis means that if an employee has exhausted their entitlement they have to wait until the start of the next 12-month period before their company sick pay entitlement recommences.

Maintaining regular contact.
A common misconception that I often hear from SME owners is that employees can't be contacted whilst they're sick, particularly in longer-term sickness cases. This is a myth. In fact, in my CIPD studies we were taught that employees who maintain greater contact with their employer generally return to work quicker.
https://www.mensura.be/en/client-portal/news/staying-in-touch-with-employees-on-long-term-sick-leave-is-a-good-thing

The absence policy should be clear on employee's obligations regarding communication of their illness to the employer. They need to be contacting the designated person by phone by a specific time, not by text message or email. Your policy may allow communication by means other than a phone call, however I would caution against this as a phone call is the best way of both maintaining contact with the employee and establishing the real extent of the employee's illness. Text messages, voicemails and emails are sometimes considered 'too easy' a method for employees to use to inform managers of their absence. Ideally, you are aiming to deter frequent short-term absences so making absence reporting by phone as the only acceptable method can act as a small deterrent.

With this in mind, failing to call in and follow the notification procedures should be considered as misconduct and this should be dealt with separately to managing someone for reoccurring absences.

It's important to train your managers on:

- What the policy says and ensure they understand their part in upholding the policy to achieve consistency but more importantly understand that it can act as a deterrent to bogus absenteeism.
- What action to take if an individual doesn't follow the requirement to call at the right time or even fails to call at all, as this is handled differently from someone who follows the notification procedure but still has a high rate of absenteeism.
- The questions to ask.
- How to record the absence.

Here are some basic questions managers could be trained to ask in the event they take a call from someone calling in sick:

- When did you start feeling ill?
- What are your symptoms?
- Have you conducted a doctor?
- Will you be getting a doctor's appointment?
- Do you expect to be in tomorrow?
- Is there any work or urgent actions that need attending to?

In the case of an employee failing to follow the appropriate procedures continuously (after the procedures have been explained to them) – for instance they're getting their mum to phone in or they're just not phoning at all, or perhaps sending a text at ten o'clock and the policy says a phone call is needed by eight o'clock – you can invoke a disciplinary hearing for failing to follow company absence notification procedures.

To ensure that any disciplinary action arising from the hearing is applied correctly, you will need to ensure that your own disciplinary procedures are correctly followed and remember to at least follow the ACAS Code of Practice which includes:

- Write to the employee 48 hours in advance of your proposed hearing, giving them the right to be accompanied.
- State the allegation in the letter and also include any evidence you have.
- State clearly that the disciplinary warning is related to misconduct i.e. the failure to follow procedures not the absence itself so the employee isn't drawn into thinking they are being penalised for being sick.

Obviously there will be limited circumstances where an employee is unable to follow the procedures – hospitalisation, for example, or complete loss of voice – but remember they are limited and I have never heard of a company wishing to invoke disciplinary or attendance management procedures against an employee who has been hospitalised or been severely ill.

If the outcome goes against the employee despite any representations or excuses the employee makes at the hearing, I would normally expect that a first stage written warning (sometime referred to as verbal written warning) be issued at that point. The key points to making this a valid warning is to follow your own procedures. It would be truly ironic if a warning for not following procedures was overturned because procedures weren't followed!

MANAGING SHORT-TERM ABSENCES

Handling frequent short-term absences.

If you describe yourself as having a short-term absence problem this is probably due to frequent sporadic absences from a small number of employees. The odd Monday and Friday, maybe a few days during the week i.e. short spells of absence. Often the reasons given for these absences are: a sore head, sickness, diarrhoea, sore throat, colds, flus and the like.

I would advise implementing a monitoring process to deter the short-term absence 'holiday club' – those individuals with increasingly frequent absences on Mondays and Fridays particularly but also days off during the week. The monitoring process is conducted by managers in friendly, but firm, return-to-work interviews with the employee on their return to the workplace. This means the employee cannot simply come back to work and pretend that nothing happened and that nobody noticed that they were away. They'll know that they will return to a face-to-face meeting with their manager and will need to detail all of their symptoms. If the symptoms are genuine, the return-to-work interview will be straightforward. If the employee is abusing the system, or they only felt marginally under the weather, the return-to-work interview will make life that bit harder for them and knowing that they face that interview each time they return is likely to reduce their absence overall. Have a return-to-work interview template that is filled in each time an absence occurs. At https://www.solvehr.co.uk/no_employment_lawyer_required/ there are a number of helpful templates that you can download for free. Here you will find a return-to-work interview template form that you can use to take them through the interview process.

I strongly recommend that you do these interviews, not only as a deterrent but also because you will then have evidence of the conversation that took place – it can support your consideration for the wellbeing of the employee and their fitness to return to work and any other issues which might come from the conversation. Published CIPD statistics over the last 10 years show that companies who conduct return to work interviews tend to experience a reduction in sickness absence. After conducting the interview, log the absence so that you can start to get a clearer picture of any pattern.

Should a pattern of frequent absence arise, you will be in a position to talk to them and be able to highlight at the earliest opportunity that the absence is unacceptable – this is the key to effectively managing absence. In your talk with them, you can summarise along these lines: "Well, you know, this is the *Nth* absence you've had in this period. This is your return-to-work form from last week; this is the one from three months ago; this is the one from four months ago; and what I'm seeing here is that there might be a problem."

Because absence can be quite emotive, as it is obviously personal, an employee may naturally already be on the defensive replying "I've been a fabulous employee for fifteen years, never had a day off sick; now I'm having a bad year, and all of a sudden you're down my throat..." Obviously the approach you take with the long-standing, having-a-rough-year employee might be slightly different to that taken with the individual who has only been in the business a short while but has had four days off in the last month. In fact, in the case of the latter, you should really be seriously considering if you want them in your employment especially if you believe their illnesses to be exaggerated or false.

Deal with absence issues as consistently as possible, delivering the key message to employees that their level of absence in particular is unsustainable for the business. Keep reminding the employee that together you're running a business, delivering a service, creating a product and every day that they're off has an impact. It impacts their other colleagues and it impacts the company's ability to hit targets which is why you have to manage absence tightly across the company. Explain that they're not being picked out, they're not being made a scapegoat, it's not that you disbelieve their absence or are calling them a liar (extremely sticky ground, unless you have evidence to the contrary and increasingly the likes of Facebook can supply this evidence) but that absence in general is bad for the business. State that what you are doing is monitoring absence levels and this approach is applicable to everybody when they're absent.

A good absence policy:

- will have a trigger system, for example, three instances of absence in a rolling 12-month period triggers a formal absence review meeting (not the return-to-work meeting) with a member of management and an HR representative. In the review meeting reiterate the point above that absence is bad for the business.
- will have a system of absence management meetings (or capability meetings as the next best option) that mirrors the Advisory, Conciliation and Arbitration Service (ACAS) Code of Practice.
- is not the same as your disciplinary policy. Managing illness through a disciplinary process doesn't go down well in employment tribunals or with the employees themselves. Naturally and inevitably, in a disciplinary hearing the employee feels that they're being punished for potentially uncontrollable events – they can't help themselves being sick, is normally the cry that we hear.

Having absence hearings removes any potentially contentious tone of the meetings in the initial stages. In my experience, these meetings focus more on supporting the individual, as well as explaining the unacceptable pattern and measures the company will take as a result.

So, quite simply, good management is the answer to managing short-term absence, which involves being firm, fair and consistently following up with employees when they're sick. Of course, there are always going to be exceptions to the rule where employees may be suffering from an underlying condition which results in an absence pattern and thus they are likely to be protected under the Equality Act 2010. Just for completeness, a disability in the Equality Act 2010 is defined as something that would be perceived to affect somebody's ability to complete day-to-day activities, which might include, dressing, walking, getting up in the morning, shopping etc. and that the condition has had a lasting effect normally defined as 12-months or more.

Because of this wide definition, conditions to be mindful of are dyslexia, depression or anxiety – note that 'stress' is not normally included in this definition. You need to exercise caution and be wary about employee, GP and Occupational health judgements on a condition. Case law outcomes make it clear that the employer has a duty to satisfy themselves about an employee's condition. This is fundamental if a dismissal has been made for absence reasons. To reiterate, it is for the employer to decide whether they consider the employee disabled or not. You are required to look at the evidence and make sure that you have done thorough investigations, which may well include health reports.

Protection for underlying conditions.

Underlying conditions that could be considered as disabilities are afforded protection in law. In any correspondence, welfare meeting or indeed absence hearing that you have with an employee it is important that you demonstrate that you are making reasonable adjustments to allow for an underlying condition.

So, how can you manage short-term absence and an underlying condition? Let's look at an example of an employee who has communicated to the business that they are suffering from Coeliac's disease. This affects the intestine and results in symptoms that include diarrhoea, abdominal pain and bloating, often with frequent levels of absence. The typical pattern of such an employee's absence history could look as follows:

a) 3 days diarrhoea
b) 1 day migraine
c) 5 days cold and flu
d) 2 days stomach pains
e) 1 day migraine
f) 3 days stomach pain

It is important when having the hearing to discount from the above pattern any absence related to Coeliac's disease, as this is a reasonable adjustment, and instead focus on absences related to colds, flu and headaches, because they are not considered to be an underlying condition. The employee may seek to make an argument about the effect of the Coeliac's disease on their immunity as an excuse for the other absences, however, that is for you to decide if you accept that argument and perhaps task an occupational health professional with answering that question for you.

Allowing for absences that could be attributed to an employee's disability shows you are making a 'reasonable adjustment' as required by law. However not all absences may be attributable to the employee's disability and you are quite within your rights to monitor and record these unattributable absences. The employee is protected over matters relating to their disability but every absence does not need to be ignored or go unrecorded. Quite the opposite. You should still continue to monitor absence for all employees consistently, although your tone of discussions might be different where someone has an underlying condition. You can also ask questions about how they are managing their condition and how they are supporting themselves which can help to mitigate against absence. You might ask the following questions:

- Have they had advice to adapt or change their diet? Are they doing so? Are they eating healthily?
- What advice have they been given on mitigating illness? Have they been advised to get flu inoculations, have they had the time to do this?

These kinds of questions can be asked sensitively and give an opportunity to point out to them again that the absence level cannot be sustained for the business. It can often start a dialogue about other reasonable adjustments you might be willing to make. These adjustments could improve the employee's health and ultimately reduce absence, such as:

- Longer breaks to attend the gym at lunch.
- Time off to get a flu jab.
- Getting a microwave so healthier food can be reheated.
- Changing the toilet facilitates to give greater privacy.

And if you're prepared to make reasonable adjustments you can then quite validly in turn expect to hold them accountable to their commitments and actions to improve absence. Whether those be eating healthier, getting counselling or going to the gym more frequently. Ensure you make these key outcomes clear. But do ensure you clarify, regardless of whether you are issuing a warning or not, what improvement in attendance levels the employee should make. Are you looking for them to have a clean record for the next three months? For the next six months? Are they allowed one further absence? Reiterate the provisions to improve their well-being you agreed and where or not you believe a referral to occupational health is appropriate.

Another consideration that you need to be prepared for is that the absence could be a direct or indirect result of stress at work. An employee might come to you and say their Coeliac's disease has flared up and that tends to happen when they are stressed.

It would be worthwhile then looking at putting a stress plan in place* This might include scheduling regular meetings to discuss their health situation and stressors to ensure that the company's being proactive. You might collect health information prior to employees starting in employment with you. (Note it is unlawful to ask for this information before appointment.) Firstly note the changing data obligations on processing and storing this data, The General Data Processing Regulations, however, if you do and you ask questions on stress and depression, this can be helpful in defending a claim that an employee later might try to make that their job or manager caused them anxiety and stress. Particularly where an employee does declare this is a pre-existing condition. Bearing in mind once an employee does make a declaration you are duty bound to make reasonable adjustments to accommodate. 'Reasonable adjustments' is a term that has been around for some time and its meaning was consolidated in the Equality Act 2010. Making a reasonable adjustment means it is your obligation as an employer to physically adjust the workplace or a policy or practice that your company has to ensure you don't disadvantage workers or applicants who are disabled. 'Disability' includes physical and mental conditions that affect a person's ability to live everyday life normally. This might include allowing the employee to be accompanied by a carer or family member for welfare meetings, discounting absences related to hospital appointments for their condition and so on.

If they're sick – they're sick!

A major advisory point to note when managing absence is do not fall into the trap of allowing employees to take a holiday in the event that they are phoning in sick. If they're sick, they're sick. The practice of taking a holiday might help you in the short term if they have holidays to take but it won't help longer term. Certainly in my experience, if you allow it to happen once or twice, employees will continually do this. Then what happens is you can't plan your workload, putting a strain on other employees; before you know it, another staff member will phone up also saying, "I'm not feeling very well but I've got holidays to take. Can I take them as holidays?" If you allow one to do it, everyone's allowed to do it. So I would strongly recommend you don't allow this practice.

In terms of proactively dealing with the sporadic Monday/Friday club, where somebody's got a hangover because they've been watching their football the night before, the best way to tackle this is to anticipate bad behaviour and send out communications prior to major events. If you know the Euros or the World Cup are on, it's reasonable to suspect there will be a lot of drinking being done. There are two approaches here: the formal and the goodwill.

In the formal approach, put out a communication to make it very clear what the company policy or view would be if somebody was to 'pull a sicky' because of a hangover, regardless of the importance of the match, as you are not the type of company that can accommodate one-off changes for health and safety or production reasons. Be clear and communicate why unfortunately you can't be lenient and that you are not trying to be a kill joy but do require employees to be considerate to their employment obligations. Also be very clear about the manager's role in managing these situations.

The goodwill approach might be to embrace the situation (if one-off changes for health and safety and production can be made) be encouraging and let staff come to work by noon. View it as an opportunity to capture some goodwill amongst the workforce.

Top tips for managing short-term absences:

1. Put in a system or procedure to measure absences using a trigger or Bradford Factor system. The Bradford Factor is a calculation of the relationship between number of absences and the length of the absences.
2. Look for regular patterns in the absences.
3. Do return to work interviews: this allows both the employee and the manager to agree a formal record of the absence, the reasons for it and whether there are any underlying conditions to take account of.
4. Be consistent and follow through.
5. Treat everyone the same regardless or you lose your credibility.
6. Take the warning system outside of the 'Disciplinary' Process.
7. Use occupational health companies that actually give useful information and understand the challenges of being an employer.

MANAGING LONG-TERM ABSENCE

Early and regular communication.

Long-term absence is normally defined as an absence of over four weeks or longer. Often this type of absence comes out of the blue, where somebody has maybe had a fall, broken their leg, or all of a sudden has crumbled under the pressures of life and gone to the doctor to get a sick line. Early intervention is generally accepted within HR professional circles to reduce and minimise the length of long-term absences. A good early intervention strategy normally entails regular communication with the employee.

Oftentimes it can be easy to take the approach of "Oh, the sick line expires in four weeks' time; we'll wait and see what happens then," and you put it to the back of your mind, doing nothing about it.

However, the best approach is to speak to the employee, ideally as soon as you know there will be a long-term absence, and then every week thereafter throughout the four weeks they're off.

Offer support to the individual and find out what the actual issues are. Doctors' lines can be notoriously unhelpful in terms of defining what an employee is actually off with. Sometimes they are used to cover an absence which might not even be due to illness but instead bereavement for family issues. Ones to watch for, obviously, are:

- Stress at work.
- Depression related to work.
- Anxiety related to work.

When any of those types of conditions are stated in a sick line you need to really get on it as quickly as possible. When I say 'on it' what I mean is be ready and prepared to do any or all of the following:

- a referral to an Occupational Health professional on the basis of the sick line.
- potentially speaking with managers to make them aware of the issue.
- and looking into the idea of putting a stress-at-work action plan in place.

It almost sounds like I am recommending the antithesis of what you should be doing if you've got a case of stress in the business. Your more natural instinct as a manager or owner might be to leave well alone and minimise any contact with an employee, either out of respect or to avoid rocking the boat. However, upon receiving a doctor's line, your duty of care to the employee is such that you need to show that you are taking conscious measures to mitigate any stress at work or alleviate any symptoms of stress. Doing so will protect your business in the event of a tribunal.

When you get these lines which say 'stress at work,' it can potentially be incredibly frustrating for managers or yourself. You can feel, personally, that it's an unfair diagnosis by the doctor or that the employee has been less than genuine in their complaints, particularly if the absence is on the back of a negative performance management review or some disciplinary hearing they have been called for. Regardless of your personal feelings, the issue is that as soon as the sick line card has been played, you have to deal with it. And dealing with it might be as simple as trying to change the employee's perceptions of what was happening at work prior to their absence. So often we get this kind of knee-jerk reaction from employees when they are being more tightly managed, or when a new manager comes on board, and their stress at work is actually just a reflection of the changes occurring and a reflection of their feelings of being unsettled. Sometimes taking the time to explain changes or understand their feelings can help.

It may not be the change in duties, it might be because they've been asked to justify what work they're doing on a day-to-day basis and that they can't provide satisfactory evidence. You can then explain in turn that it's just good management practice to monitor how employees spend their time, and ensure that they are working efficiently. If they have not been asked these kinds of questions before or are not used to having to document their activities, being asked to do so can cause them stress. In this kind of case, work with the employee. Explain the reasons for the way that you are dealing with them, justify your need for the evidence or information and reiterate the business' determination to support the employee.

In managing a long-term absence, at the earliest indication that it may happen, agree upfront with the employee, whilst communication between you is still at its strongest, the pattern and frequency of contact between them and the company during their absence. You might ask them to phone in every two weeks just to confirm that they're OK, or you might call them every two weeks just to check in and let them know what's going on in the business. These calls are an expectation – in other words, if they don't stick to this pattern of contact they're not playing ball. Ideally follow this up in an email or in writing to confirm with them that this is how communication will be managed and that this is the company's expectations of them over this time (especially if it's not already in a policy), justifying this level of interaction by reiterating the company's general policy or requirements to communicate with staff during long-term absence. By communicating with them from the outset you avoid the risk of losing contact with them, and also avoid the difficulty of then requesting and establishing regular communications several weeks down the line when they may have become used to the lack of contact. Worse still, without regular communications from the outset, the absent employee may start to feel isolated and resentful. Then when a call does come they may think, "You've left me to my own devices for this long, what's the problem now all of a sudden? You don't care, all you want is to get me back to work; all you want is for me to sign the doctor's report..." This may make them less amenable to cooperating with Occupational Health reports. So do start as you mean to continue!

Spelling out their cooperation obligations from the start means that the employee can more clearly recognise that failing to follow their part of the bargain may result in a different conversation entirely.

Input from medical professionals.

The best thing to do when dealing with any mental health condition cited on a doctor's line, is to ideally get an Occupational Health (OH) referral, or to request a report from the employee's GP directly. Doing at least one of these can offer a number of benefits.

Following the employee's consultation by the chosen medical professional, the business can ask a number of well-worded, specific questions to the assessing physician about what measures the business can take to support the individual and what timescale the individual is likely to be off for. You can ask the doctor or physician what they feel the cause of the stress at work is and how they feel stress at work is manifesting itself. You can also ask what duties the employee may be able to perform on any return to work and what duties and interactions the employee does not feel confident in or has concerns about doing. Often this will help to mitigate risk and to further conversations with the employee about their return to work.

Cost may be a factor in choosing an OH referral over requesting a letter from the GP. Typically OH referrals cost between £150 and £450 depending on the practitioner and the level of service, whilst GP letters could be free; some surgeries though are increasingly requesting that employers pay for the privilege of seeing a report on their employee, and this can be £60-100. In the event the surgery does charge you may be better choosing the OH report instead. You're going to get a lot more value from the process as a good occupational health provider should be quicker and specialises in determining the employee's fitness for work. They will generally be more pragmatic and helpful about the employee's return, detailing the likelihood and likely return-to-work date.

However, there may not scope for an occupational health referral, either because your company policy specifically demands a doctor's report, or there are cost constraints in which case I would certainly pursue the avenue of a letter from the GP. You may request a report on the condition directly from the employee's GP yourself (after asking the employee's permission to do so). The employee will first need to complete and sign an 'Access to Medical Records' request form*, which explains their right to refuse their consent to a medical report. A good form will also explain their rights in terms of how the process will work; it also outlines that they have the right to see the report prior to it coming to you. If you need a signature for an Access to Medical Records request form, have the form to hand and give the employee a copy of the letter that you might be sending to their doctor or the Occupational Health referral form for them to sign off. Even give them a stamped, addressed envelope, in the event that they don't want to sign the form and give it back to you there and then. Make it as easy as possible for them to take the next steps and comply with the communication pattern that you wish to establish.

Some doctors can be slippery when it comes to writing reports so I would suggest you get a really well-worded letter drafted with strong specific questions to be answered, otherwise a generic report comes back, which will be a waste of time and money. Remember to attach a job description to any request for an Occupational Health or doctor's report, because it will give the doctor or specialist much more information and allow them to challenge - in a kind and reasonable way - the employee's complaints in the context of their work and to determine if they truly are unfit for work. In addition, and most importantly, it can really support in advising you of any reasonable adjustments the business might be able to make for the employee to give them the confidence or support to come back to do their job. Better still, when writing the letter completing the form in the first instance, you might be able to propose your own reasonable adjustments that you're willing to make, instead of asking the doctor to think of adjustments for themselves. Ask them to confirm whether they feel that the individual would be able to do the job if the proposed amendments to their duties were made. These amendments are likely to cover a temporary period until the employee is completely recovered or eased back in and able to fulfil the original remit of their job again.

More often than not you will also have to be persistent in pursuing the report and push secretaries/receptionists and remind doctors. It really depends on the surgery and doctor. Some doctors are great and come back to you quickly, and if you've asked them quite specific questions they may give you a fairly detailed response. However, on average it can be four to twelve weeks to get a report back.

In the case of an Occupational Health referral, you should complete a form, normally the occupational health providers' form, which states the length and absence of the illness and has a few boxes for you to check in terms of the answers you are looking for from the occupational health specialist. Sometimes your employee can sign this same form. This is then received by the occupational health specialist who is reviewing your employee and an appointment is made. Quite often these appointments are conducted by phone, unless the case is more complex or absence has been prolonged. After the employee has been assessed you will receive a report, normally two to three pages, which should address all the questions you have asked in your form and give you an insight into the absence issues with recommendations for any support you can offer and indeed actions the employee should take themselves to improve their chances of returning to work quicker.

How long will they be off?

Below are guidelines on how long you should expect absence from work to be, summarising the general length of a recovery for a specific condition, or operation.

Table 2: Maximum and Minimum Expected duration of absence (in weeks):

Operation required	**Minimum absence**	**Maximum absence**
Angiography/Angioplasty	<1	4
Appendectomy (appendix)	1-2 (keyhole)	2-3 open
Arthroscopy (a tiny camera in a joint)	<1	<1
Cataract Surgery (eyes)	2	4
Cholecystectomy (gall bladder)	2-3 (keyhole)	3-5 (open)
Colposcopy cautery (women's procedure)	<1	<1
CABG (heart bypass surgery/heart valve surgery)	4	8
Cystoscopy (looks at the bladder)	<1	<2
D& C (women's minor operation)	<1	<1
ERPC (camera looking at the small bowel area)	<1	<1
Femoro-popliteal graft (replacing an artery in leg)	4	12
Haemorrhoid banding (tying, not cutting, operation)	<1	<1
Haemorrhoidectomy	2	4

Operation required	Minimum absence	Maximum absence
Hysterectomy	3 (keyhole)	7 (open)
Hernia – one side operated on	1-2 keyhole	2-3 (open)
Hernia – both sides operated on	1-2 (keyhole)	6
Laparoscopy (sterilisation)	<1	<1
Laparotomy (opening up the abdomen)	6	12
Mastectomy (breast operation, usually for cancer)	2	6
Pacemaker insertion (may need time off, while working, to change wound dressing)	<1	<1
Pilonidal sinus (boil near the bottom, may need time off, while working, to change dressing)	<1	<1
Retinal detachment (eye ball lining)	<1	Avoid heavy work for life
Total hip or knee replacement	12	26
TURP (prostate operation)	2	5
TOP (termination of pregnancy)	<1	<1
Vasectomy	<1	<1

Taken from 'EEF Managing Sickness Absence' 2007. Referenced, Oxford Handbook of General Practice, 2nd edition, (p199) by Simon, Chantal, Everitt, Hazel (2005)

Getting them back in the job.

One part of the puzzle is of course the human condition: the mind is very adept at talking its owner out of being productive! If we're getting paid to sit at home and watch TV, it's easier to do that than getting up for work every day even if it means being bored, feeling sorry for ourselves or simply not facing reality. Inevitably, there are some individuals who will find it harder to get back into the mind-set of coming back to work.

Often if an absence is a result of a disagreement at work or a breakdown of a relationship with a manager or colleague – of which you may or may not be aware of – naturally there is a huge reluctance and fear about returning to work, so it's definitely worth bearing in mind all of these different psychological factors when coaching someone back to work. In addition, one very successful method that I have found for managing long-term absence is home visits.

Make sure again that your policy or your terms and conditions allow for a home visit; outline that that is a reasonable expectation and that employees are required to cooperate. It doesn't actually have to be in the employee's home if either of you feel uncomfortable with that, but it can be a measure for how cooperative the employee is willing to be about their return to work.

In a tribunal situation if you can show that you've done as much as you could to maintain dialogue between an absent employee and the business, and that it's the employee that has impeded that dialogue by refusing a home visit or an off-site visit, it shows your reasonableness and their lack of cooperation. In any case, a home visit can be really fruitful because it has the ability to repair relationships. The employee feels more at ease in their own environment potentially with a spouse, parent, or even child around them which is comforting.

Provided you've chosen a representative from the business who is willing to listen, who is compassionate, who reiterates that the purpose of the visit is to support the employee, and who asks questions about how a return to work can be achieved without being pushy, you can often get a really strong result. You can find out or at least get a much better idea of how long the absence might continue for, and what the real reasons for the absence might be. Feeling more secure in their own environment and having had the benefit of time, they might be ready to disclose to the representative any breakdown in relationships or grievances they have.

In addition, you are likely to be able to gauge more clearly how genuine the absence is at this stage. We've been to home visits often, and have seen, for instance, an employee who's been off for six to eight months after a major operation, who says they're still not fit to come back because of low mobility and, even though there's nobody else there to provide assistance, their house is immaculate! This doesn't mean jumping to huge conclusions – they could have a cleaner, you don't know their personal circumstances – but often your gut instinct in these situations is right. It can be a really good barometer for how the employee really feels. Are they just pushing out their absence a bit longer or do they seriously have an issue that needs to be resolved?

Home visits can be really useful and there is absolutely nothing to be afraid of when requesting one. If you do go for a home visit, be prepared: think about the questions you want to ask; think about the language you're going to use and come prepared with any documents you may need that haven't already been completed.

What if they won't come back?

What if you can't get the employee back to work? They might not be able, or interested in returning to work. In that case you're probably looking at a capability dismissal - that's where having a capability policy, as mentioned earlier in this chapter, or an absence management policy, is so key because it's their inability to work (not any misconduct) that leads you to dismiss them.

With an ill-health termination, you need to show that you've followed all the formal steps, that you've made the necessary reasonable adjustments, and that you've followed through with the suggestions from any reports. I would be really reluctant to make any dismissal without the benefit of a report from a medical adviser. You will need to show that you've taken every reasonable step and tried to gather as much information and evidence on whether this employee should be dismissed before making that decision. This reduces any risk of a tribunal.

The other thing to try and factor in when someone is off long term and you are considering dismissal for ill health is does the employee want you to terminate them? What do they stand to gain by that? This is a point that is often overlooked. Many employees, or ex-employees, know the system, or they've heard from family or friends about what they would be entitled to on benefits (certainly in this day and age, that's much less than it would have been a few governments ago, but regardless, there are still disability benefits out there and people exercise them). There are also insurance policies, personal or company policies, to consider. The absent employee may have surmised that in the event they're unable to work, claiming benefits would be equal to or even better than the income of working.

Look at their home circumstances. Has their daughter, or wife, just had a baby? Do they have high travel costs? Are there stress issues? Have they disclosed previously that they intend to start their own mini-business? Have they got a qualification that could see them into a job elsewhere that they might prefer? There are many factors to consider. I'm don't mean to infer that everybody is dishonest or trying to manipulate the benefits system, but at the end of the day this book is written for you, the business owner, and we live in the real world. Evaluating people's motivations in these circumstances can be very worthwhile and will allow you to have frank discussions and find solutions rather than wasting a lot of time going through an unnecessary and unwanted procedure.

Now the pressure may be on you to make the next move, as the employee has failed to communicate, or has indicated new problems that further postpone their return to work, or even because they know if they resign they won't be able to claim benefits. Despite the pressure, take your time to ensure you act properly and thoroughly. Weigh up all the circumstances. This could be an opportunity to choose a settlement agreement to close the case down and prevent any future claim. Your course of action might hinge on your sick pay policy and the contract of employment. Or it could come down to a commercial decision: it may be cheaper to close off an employment relationship with a settlement than paying sick pay for another six months and taking the time to guide them through a comprehensive but ultimately futile process in the hope they will return to work.

A termination dismissal for capability is normally the culmination of a number of capability warnings, and might be compounded with advice that there's no reasonable adjustments the company can feasibly afford to make, leaving you no option but to consider a termination for capability. The 'reasonable adjustments' that the legislation requires, are exactly that, 'reasonable'. You as a company must perceive the adjustments to be affordable and sensible. So for an example, if an employee is willing and able to return to work and resume full-time hours Monday to Friday, but in order to do so would need a ramp to allow them access to the premises, if the cost of putting in a ramp is prohibitive to the SME, it may be deemed more reasonable to terminate the employee than for the ramp to be installed. However, if you are faced with this type of issue you should probably take further advice as you will likely find that there is funding available to support businesses with the cost of adding assisted access for disabled people and therefore any dismissal without proper investigation could be unlawful.

Changing hours of work is likely to be a reasonable adjustment provided it's clear that it's for a temporary period only, and giving specific business reasons that any ongoing adjustments to hours will not be manageable long-term. Any refusal to make adjustments must be realistic and justified. Bear in mind, it's in your interests to show a genuine willingness to get the employee back to work which at the very least will protect yourself further in the event of a tribunal claim for discrimination, even if your efforts are not reciprocated or believed to be of any use by the employee.

To outline the value that Occupational Health reports can be, we've actually had one report that said the employee is better to be in work given the issues that they'd disclosed. It went so far to say that being back in the workplace would rebuild their confidence. Despite conveying that report to the employee, she still went on to have sporadic attendance, claiming stress at work as the cause. In that case, given that the advisor has clearly outlined a position which is at odds with the employee's behaviour, the best thing you can do is look at a potential termination and have confidence in your decision given the report findings. You are not obliged to follow the Health advisor's advice in the report to the letter, though the report is likely to contain valuable information and ignoring it could be reckless.

However, do remember the law allows you as the employer to take decisions on the basis of reasonable investigation and advice and weigh up the employee's requirements with your needs as a business. Say, for instance, an Occupational Health company has been supporting your business for a year, and has recently submitted a report on an employee who's been in and out of long-term sickness for the last six years. The report says the employee should be able to come back to work in 4 weeks' time. You might take a reasonable commercial decision that says "Given the pattern of absence and the history with this individual, the business does not necessarily believe, despite the report, that the employee will be able to come back in four weeks. As this has been on-going for 6 years it has become unsustainable for the business to manage the situation any further. Therefore we are making a decision to terminate this individual." You've sought and listened to professional healthcare advice, but ultimately you've made a reasonable decision based on commercial factors that correctly overrides the advice.

Conclusion.

We've covered various scenarios surrounding long-term absence and highlighted some of the pitfalls. The key to protecting your business is to be prepared: have a plan that you follow closely, document everything, have official consultations with relevant professionals, and to keep communication with the absentee as strong as possible. And in any extreme or unusual circumstances, always get a second opinion from a healthcare provider. However, don't be afraid to take a commercial decision!

Ideally, after a four-week absence you want to starting putting a little pressure on the employee to give you an indication of whether they're coming back to work or not. If, as recommended above, a conversation took place upfront and expectations on communication were all laid out from the get-go, this will be far easier. The input from doctors or Occupational Health can add value to this conversation. Additionally, this information (omitting anything confidential) may be fed back into planning meetings for work allocation with reduced resource and can help prevent colleagues become frustrated with how long the sick member of staff has been off for.

Top tips for managing long-term absence:

1. Engage early and set the communication standards for ongoing contact.
2. Find a good occupational health service.
3. Never ignore work related reasons absence/sickness written on a doctor's certificate.
4. Ask for permission for a doctor's or occupational health specialist to report.
5. Use home visits to improve relations, anticipate returns and speed things along.
6. Be prepared at a home visit have all the documents you require signed or reviewed handy to present. Go with a stamped addressed envelope.
7. Put yourself in the shoes of the employee and note the signs and signals they are giving you. What do they really want given the circumstances?

6

MAKING WORK, WORK: MANAGING WORK AND EMPLOYEES' HOME LIFE

INCREASING legislation on leave makes it incredibly difficult for employers to stay up to date on the latest entitlements afforded to employees. There is now leave for parents sharing maternity leave (called Shared Parental Pay and Leave); additional paternity leave was scrapped as a result and statutory bereavement leave for the death of the child will be introduced as will rights for grandparents who have caring duties. This is an area that government can make quick wins in so legislation can change so I do caution you to double check government websites for up-to-date information when you get a request that may at first seem out of the ordinary. Below is an overview of the most common types of leave entitlement.

New Babies: Maternity, Paternity and Shared Parental Pay and Leave.

What should you do if your employee notifies you that she is pregnant? Very little, actually, in the initial stages of pregnancy. The first step is to do a pregnancy risk assessment on https://www.solvehr.co.uk/no_employment_lawyer_required/ and to make any possible amendments or reasonable adjustments to the role they are doing. This is to ensure the mother and foetus are not exposed to any harm in the workplace as well as protecting your business and making sure that you have the proper health and safety paperwork in place.

At twenty-six weeks of pregnancy, the pregnant employee will be given their Mat-B1 certificate, normally issued by their midwife. When your employee hands you this certificate you have the proper confirmation of the pregnancy and the employee's due date. At this point you can start having discussions with the employee around their plans.

From an employment law perspective it is worth noting that an employee doesn't automatically qualify for maternity pay although they do automatically qualify for maternity leave. This is an important distinction in terms of calculations on maternity pay and leave.

Initially, I'm going to deal with maternity leave. A woman has the right to fifty-two weeks of maternity leave to care for her baby, from the date of birth. In the first twenty-six weeks of the fifty-two the employee is considered to be on 'ordinary maternity leave' where she has the right to return to her job in its entirety – the one that she left. Then the employee may have a further twenty-six weeks of 'additional maternity leave' where the company does not need to guarantee that the job will still be there, but they do need to guarantee the individual that they are able to return to a job of the same or similar standing and salary.

To be eligible for statutory maternity pay (SMP), the employee has to have worked for your company for twenty-six weeks by the fifteenth week before the day that they are due. So working backwards, if they were due on the 1st October, fifteen weeks before that is 18th June – therefore she would need to have been employed on or before the 18th December of the previous year to qualify. If your contracts or policies are more generous, in this example the start of employment date can be later than the 18th December.

Presently statutory maternity legislation affords the employee six weeks at 90% of pay unless that is less than the statutory rate, in which case the statutory rate applies, and then a further thirty-three weeks at the statutory rate. The statutory rate changes every year (check correct figures on the government's website) and is sitting presently at just under £140 per week. If an employee does not meet the eligibility criteria (i.e. the length of service stipulated above) the employee can claim Maternity Allowance by completing a form and making an application through the job centre or online. This will normally afford the employee payment directly from the government at the statutory rate for the 39 weeks.

Obviously you are entitled as a business owner to adjust your maternity pay and leave provisions to pay more if you feel it fits your organisation, culture and ideals, but the statutory is the minimum obligations you need to pay. You can reclaim maternity payments from the government if your company is eligible – normally if you are an SME below a certain revenue threshold – your accountant should be able to advise on this.

Once you've received the employee's Mat-B1 and they have made you aware of their intentions regarding when their maternity leave might start and how long they intend taking, it's good practice to confirm this with them in writing. The letter should cover the maternity period, their payments and the required notice if they were to decide to change their intended return-to-work date. Normally, good employers are having conversations and keeping in touch with their employees who are having babies in the intervening time. The legislation also affords for up to 10 paid 'keeping in touch' days (often referred to as KIT days) to the women on maternity leave. This is where the employee is allowed to come back into the workplace and either do their own job, or a job of a similar nature, should they wish. The aim of this is to enable the employee to keep their hand in, see their peers and understand what's going on in the company. It is generally considered a great way of re-engaging knowledgeable employees and inspiring and supporting them in being prepared to come back to the workplace.

Paternity pay and leave.

Paternity pay has similar eligibility factors to maternity pay, in that you're only required to pay a 'father' – there are various definitions of a father (including partner, spouse etc.) – if they have worked for you for six months, by the fifteenth week before the estimated date of childbirth. If they've worked with you for long enough they'll be eligible for pay of two weeks – again at the current SMP rate which is the same rate normally as the statutory maternity pay rate.. And they have to take those weeks in week blocks (either one block of two weeks, or two blocks of one week are permissible), and pay and leave can only legitimately commence after the baby is born.

Shared Parental Pay and Leave.

Shared parental pay and leave is something that's been recently introduced, and this as where the mum and dad of a new child, or a baby not yet born, have opted for the maternity pay and or leave that is normally entitled to a mother to be passed over to the father or partner of the mother. This is more likely to happen when the employing organisation of one parent has better maternity/paternity arrangement's than that of the other parent, who then goes back to work whilst the parent with enhanced pay and leave terms continues the childcare.

In this case there's a fair amount of administrative requirements on all sides of the equation including the two employers. The most important thing that you should be aware of is this request can legitimately happen. A man can choose to effectively go on 'maternity leave' and take pay and leave, as a woman might do, without suffering any bias or discrimination by an employer for this choice. The couple are required to write to both employers separately and let them know that this is their request. There is a curtailment notice which is required to be completed by the mother a certain number of weeks before the baby is born and normally before the leave is due to be taken. In effect, this means the mum exits the maternity pay scheme of her employer and any periods of leave and pay fall now under 'shared parental pay and leave'.

She can opt to take these leave and pay periods in blocks – off and on, as can the father. As you can imagine, this can get pretty complex. Mum could be working, could be off for four weeks and then Dad could be off for four weeks; then mum could be back off again for six months before returning for another period. The legislation allows for a maximum of up to three blocks of either parent taking leave. You could have a yo-yo effect over this year, which may actually suit your business if you are a seasonal or term time business. Alternatively and I can hear you thinking it, more normally this could be confusing and difficult to accommodate.

Employers can refuse to accommodate a request for Shared Parental Leave if they have reasonable grounds, but your reasons have to be pretty strong and you need to be prepared to have the discrimination card played against you if you refuse. If you have a good economic reason, or perhaps a strong case against an employee coming into the workplace and then leaving it again perhaps from a consistency angle it might be worth the refusal; you would have to weight this up against how likely it would be that the employee would understand and accept your rationale, because like maternity pay and leave, shared parental pay and leave is enshrined and protected. You don't want to have any discrimination claims related to a dad or a male trying to take shared parental pay and leave and then being ridiculed or not getting the same benefit that a woman might have. There have already been a number of cases recently, where a man has asserted discrimination on the basis that men in their organisation don't have the same leave and pay for paternity as the women have for maternity. Some of these claims have been successfully won and other cases strongly defended. In the latter there was a strong argument put forth that enhanced terms for women served the organisational aim of retaining and promoting more women in a male-dominated environment. Regardless, the claims illustrate the changing of the times in employment and expectations in terms of equality.

Returning to work after family leave and changing working hours.

The issues for employers on accommodating employees' hours normally arise when the mother (or increasingly now the partner, particularly after Shared Parental Pay and Leave ShPP and ShPL see below) is coming back to the workforce and looking at their options for flexibility. Normally they are thinking in terms of having a couple of days of work balanced with bringing up their young child.

The legislation on the right to request this change to contracted hours has changed recently but not overly so. Rather than have a legal framework for the requirement to request flexible working, there is now an ACAS Code of Practice that employers are expected to use as a guide. And most notably the right to 'request' is now afforded to all employees, with or without caring responsibilities provided they have been in post over 26 weeks.

Largely, the process Code of Practice and the legislation that preceded it, requires an employee to put in writing to their employer a request to change their hours as this is a fundamental change in their contract of employment. The employer and employee should meet together to discuss the practicality of the request, particularly in the case where the employer is hesitant or doesn't believe that the request can be practically accommodated and thus is likely to have to turn down the employee's request. However, if you think that the proposal can be workable for you and your business and you want to just rubberstamp it, then a meeting might not be necessary; in this case I recommend you simply write back to the employee and accept their proposal. In any formal letter or email of confirmation make it clear that the new hours constitute a change to their contract of employment specifying the hours, the pro-rata of their new annual salary and holiday entitlements, confirm their job title and any changes in role or job-sharing requirements. Also I recommend that you consider imposing a trial period and then maybe outline any criteria for measuring success – for example clients still receive goods on time, the job share handover goes smoothly and there's no cost of lost business.

In this situation you have to be careful that you do not effectively demote an employee, particularly a maternity returner to a role that somebody else has occupied in their absence. If you're planning on keeping the temporary person in the same role that they were doing as their temporary role, when an employee is coming back to work after maternity leave, consider what roles both are going to do. Is it clear that the female employee should have her role back? What's the new reporting structure? Give some careful consideration to ensure that you're not effectively changing their role and duties then the maternity returner won't have a claim of constructive dismissal along with indirect discrimination: this claim would be on the basis that the changes have only happened due to the employee going on maternity leave, which is a direct result of their sex.

It may well be that the maternity returner's role has diminished partly due to the natural ebbs and flows of business and partly due the re-allocation of work due to their maternity leave meaning the role can now be done on a part-time basis. This may suit everyone. However, if this is not the case as the maternity returner expects to return on a full-time basis then you could look at the restructuring section of this book. Either way, I recommend that you have to have an open and honest conversation at the earliest point with the member of staff to manage their expectations and establish their intentions, which will aid in avoiding grievances or claims at a later date.

Another option available to parents and guardians is unpaid parental leave. This is not widely used but something to be aware of as an employer. It might be useful if an employee is visibly struggling to adapt to work, then suddenly becomes a single parent or has a sickly child. The law affords up to eighteen weeks unpaid entitlement, four of which can be used in any year. Normally the reasons the employee would stipulate for the request is to help settle a child into school, to spend time with a child, or to take some time off for that child. Unpaid parental leave is only afforded presently to individuals who have children and who have met the statutory criteria, unless you wish to offer more or waive the criteria. Additionally leave is required to be taken in whole week blocks and the employee has the right to return to their job without the imposition of any punitive measures for taking that time or leave entitlement.

When considering an employee's change request to a working pattern, there's always an option, particularly if you're hesitant or not sure if it's going to work for your business to agree subject to a trial. If you agree to try the change of working pattern on a trial basis, make it clear that it is a trial and communicate the agreement in writing – normally I would recommend three months to a maximum of six months – and be clear also that if the decision is that the trial has not worked (normally decided after a meeting at the end of the trial period), then the employee will be required to revert back to their normal contract of employment.

Initiating a change to hours on a trial basis is a great way to keep goodwill with the returning or requesting employee but also enables you to test the arrangement to see if it could work for your business.

Flexible working arrangements can be very wide and varied. There is the option for 'condensed hours' whereby an individual works their thirty-five or thirty-nine hours per week in a four-day week, sometimes agreeing to 'log-on' from home on the Friday. Working from home is, in itself, a flexible working arrangement that you may wish to consider for your business. Some companies fear that home-working means that employees will skive off and watch Jeremy Kyle. However, my experience is the opposite and in fact studies show that employees actually work harder because they are fearful of exactly that perception and many employees report they actually find they are more productive and motivated. One way to support and police a home working arrangement may be a remote working policy. A remote working policy can set the parameters for home working, the communication required and the recording of work conducted. Additionally, I would recommend a clause in the remote working policy to enable the business to request and require the employees back in an office environment at any time and the ability to completely revoke home or remote working if required. Unless your contracts of employment specify that the employee's place of work is their home, then there shouldn't be any issues with this, although at all times consultation would be recommended to ensure you don't in fact 'breach and newly implied term'.

The right to request flexible working extends to everybody in the workforce these days now, not just those that have children. It used to include those with caring responsibilities but now legislation affords anybody, after 26 months service, to request a change to their working hours. That could therefore include a single man or woman with no caring responsibilities but who might just be looking to pursue other projects in their day-to-day life.

So when considering a request to change the hours of a parent returning to work after leave, rather than doing so in complete isolation you could look at other verbal or written intentions your employee has alluded to. Then consider if you need a full-time role or coverage for 40 hours? Job share could be an option, particularly for lower level jobs which would ordinarily be full-time positions, for example a telephone call-centre role or a marketing administration position. You might therefore agree to create a vacancy for another part time job, or split the full-time role into two part-time positions according to duties in the roles.

Of course, you need to clearly look at the costs associated with doing this and the benefits too. There might be great benefits of retaining and engaging staff, with work done more productively and to a higher quality by sharing out a job like this. However, you are also likely to have additional costs in terms of payroll to consider: the benefits package of an extra employee to add into the cost mix, productivity losses in work handovers or 'balls being dropped' as a result of the arrangement that might be greater than would come from a single employee in the role. Again a job share could be instituted on a trial basis and is strongly recommended.

Top tips for managing family-friendly rights and leave:

1. Check the most recent legislation for entitlements – these change often.
2. Conduct a pregnancy risk assessment when you are notified of a pregnancy and again at least twice after that.
3. Approach situations involving pregnant women very cautiously.
4. Remember you could also indirectly discriminate so check your decisions are not founded on false presumptions.
5. Never refuse a change to hours without providing sound reasons as to why.
6. If you are not sure if a part time working request will work, try it on a trial basis and remember to conduct a formal review afterwards, as well as spelling out before the trial what will happen if the trial doesn't work for both parties.
7. Follow up changes to working patterns in writing – remember these are changes to the Contract of Employment.

7

EMPLOYED VERSUS CONTRACTOR STATUS:

THE DIFFERENCES BETWEEN EMPLOYING SOMEBODY AND OUTSOURCING THE WORK AND WHY IT MATTERS.

I BELIEVE that as a business owner it is important that you understand how a tribunal perceives a true employee and a true contractor and why the difference matters. The most common misconception about having a self-employed associate is that there is less risk and cost to you. This misconception can be a costly mistake that even large firms like Uber and Addison Lee have made recently. When hiring somebody, no matter how you hire them, there is a more complicated assessment that you'll need to do. Let's get into it.

There are a number of different types of employment status:

- Employed.
- Zero hour workers/employee.
- Worker.
- Casual worker.
- Agency workers.
- Self-employed individual.
- Contractor.

Management of these latter three categories are where most often organisations can unwittingly get themselves into disputes, particularly where individuals consider themselves to become part and parcel of an organisation over time.

Why would this present a problem? Normally it poses a problem where these individuals perceive that they should be entitled to the same rights that ordinary employees receive. For example, if your business experiences a downturn large enough to trigger a redundancy process, your normal employees will go through a legally-mandated redundancy consultation process. Any self-employed individuals, or contractors working at your company who are notified that their 'services are no longer required' may become aggrieved and believe that they should have been entitled to similar treatment in the situation as the normal employees. They may then allege they are being treated differently on the basis of their status.

Recently the case against Uber, the taxi-booking service illustrated this: 'self-employed' drivers successfully claimed they were effectively workers in order to gain an entitlement to holiday pay and benefits. Although at the time of writing Uber are still contesting the ruling in the European Courts, the UK Supreme Court ruling, as is stands, will clearly impose an unforeseen financial cost and obligation on Uber and any other companies in this similar position. Therefore, it is worth recognising and understanding this risk and how it may apply to your own business when you are considering the options on how to hire and engage individuals to do work for you.

The three main tests an employment judge will look at when assessing if somebody is employed by you as a worker or are indeed self-employed, are:

- Mutuality of obligation – this simply means the discretion a self-employed person has in refusing and accepting work offered to them by your company.
- Control – the more an employer tells a person what to do, and stipulates how to do it then the more likely a contract of employment exists.
- Integration.

Mutuality of obligation is probably one of the hardest to review in practical terms but is a key point in a judge's assessment of the working relationship. The types of tests that a judge will look at are as follows:

- Is the person free to refuse and accept work?
- Are there frequent breaks between periods of time that they work for you?
- Is the work for other people or companies?

- Does the 'employee' invoice?
- Do they have their own insurance?
- Do they have the right of substitution? This means in the event that they are not able to undertake the work can they instruct a colleague or friend to do the work instead?
- Do they wear a uniform - your uniform or their own branded clothes and/or personal protective equipment (PPE).
- Do you provide them with equipment and tools or do they bring their own?
- Regarding their level of expertise, how much scope do they have to determine their own tasks on the job without your interference or direction?

When you're setting up somebody as a self-employed contractor it's quite important that you establish how you intend to issue work to them and how you intend the relationship to work now, and in the future should your company increasingly rely on the individual. Remember the person beginning to work for you, on a more regular and permanent basis, has implications for the status of that person and their engagement with you.

The most simplistic example and accepted norm of the self-employed person is the original 'contract for services' arrangement: this is where your business may choose to subcontract a piece of work to another business or consultant. For example: a master builder subcontracts to a specialised trade company such as a plumber, especially for larger jobs. This arrangement is likely to be with a separate plumbing company that employs their own plumbers, meaning a commercial agreement between the parties/companies is entered into with the subcontractor invoicing for any completed work. The subcontractor will have their own insurance such as public liability insurance and professional indemnity.

A common difficulty that arises in these situations is that the subcontracted plumbing business has its own 'subbies': self-employed plumbers they hire to work on their behalf. The liability in this case rests with the plumbing business not the master contractor.

Taking a step back though if somebody:

- works with you day in, day out.
- they do not invoice you.

- you pay them (regardless of how you're paying them).
- they wear your uniform.
- you tell them where to be, at what time and what to do.
- you provide them with tools.

...then they're very likely to be found to be a worker in an Employment tribunal convened to determine their status; therefore all the statutory employment rights discussed in this book would apply to them such as such as rights to accrued holidays, continuous service, sick pay, contractual and statutory rights of unfair dismissal.

It's smart to seriously consider whether it is better to have someone in employment or somebody who is self-employed. The answer is not necessarily straightforward. The table below can help you decide:

Table 3: Employee versus Contractor Decision Criteria

Employ them if...	Contract them if...
Regular work is required day to day.	There is project work which starts and stops.
You want to be able to control their behaviour and appearance.	Specialist work which you could not necessarily direct them or challenge them on.
Recruiting these skills is easily done.	Their expertise and knowledge is expensive.
You would be concerned about their dedication to your company if they worked for someone else.	You don't mind if they work for multiple people.
It is unusual for this type of person to invoice – I would have to make up a timesheet for them.	They are used to invoicing.
I need to be able to rely upon them and for them to be able to do as they are told.	I would expect them to have insurance and a company 'established'.
They need to in one fixed location for certain hours.	They have discretion to when and where they work as long as it gets done.
They have to be trained in 'our' way.	No training is required – as a qualified person they know how to do the task.
I really only want them to do the job.	I don't mind who carries out the task.

Going back to the example of the master builder, the master builder will – regardless of who comes on site – have an obligation to everybody for very basic health and safety and inducting contractors coming onsite in health and safety practices. So don't be misled by thinking that because a master builder inducts everybody into their onsite health and safety regime, that they are then inferring employment status; this is more about the more holistic duty to protect any person walking around on-site.

However, a lot of business owners often mix up the obligations and requirements between employment law and tax law. The Construction Industry Scheme, often referred as someone having a 'CIS card' often means that an individual is mistakenly perceived as being self-employed. However, in terms of employed versus contractor status for an employment dispute, it actually comes down to the employment tribunal to make that decision; it's not contingent on how they're paid, their tax code or what the tax laws say.

Contractor status would probably be correct for a potential hire if that person can work for a number of different people, they invoice you for their services and your control of them is minimal and limited to a high level overview of the work required. A good example of a contractor is engaging a bookkeeper to manage your books: normally they will work for multiple clients; you'd expect them to know what they're doing so wouldn't need to tell them how to write up a ledger or how to create an invoice and the number of hours they work for you varies from month to month, which their invoice to you reflects.

The key takeaway from this section is to be aware how self-employed individuals may over time change their status not only in the eyes of employment law, but in their own eyes, potentially increasing your liability as an employer. There is increasing focus and discussion on the 'gig-economy' and zero-hour contracts; recent dialogue reflects an increasing perception of company exploitation of these individuals as they have no employment rights, no fixed hours and thus no security. I expect this debate to continue over the years, particularly in the context of Brexit, because there will always be a need for a flexible work force to reflect a business' peaks and troughs of trade. However, ensure you get the right labour mix for you and do not fall foul of this increasing trend of claims on employment status.

Top tips when considering contractors versus employees:

1. Consider your intention for the arrangement at the start
2. Put in an agreement to capture this.
3. Review and audit your self-employed people regularly.
4. Prepare guidelines for self-employed people or businesses with your expectations for them as self-employed people.
5. Do not be fooled into believing that tax legislation and employment legislation will arrive at the same conclusions!

□

8

RECRUITING THE BEST: THE SECRET TO GETTING THE BEST PEOPLE IN YOUR BUSINESS.

RECRUITING the best can be the difference between having an incredibly successful business with rapid growth and missing the potential growth of your business. When recruiting a new team member the best advice I can give you is to think about the values you have as a person, how they translate into your business and then how to incorporate them into your recruitment process – the business vision can generate a recruitment vision.

Job Descriptions and Personal Specifications.

A job description is essential and outlines the duties and the roles and responsibilities of the job holder. As an SME owner, you'll probably know you need an additional pair of hands, but maybe you haven't actually spent a lot of time defining the activities of the new role. In particular, what tasks are you prepared to hand over to the new recruit, initially and then later if they prove competent in the role? Often the first hire can be a book-keeper or an accounts person and that does involve giving some control over critical activities to somebody, this can be easier for some owners than others.

The personal specification, on the other hand, details the qualities and experiences that you are looking for in the successful individual coming into your organisation. This can be really helpful in the marketplace because you are defining to potential applicants not only the requirements of your role, but also the type of person you are looking for. Preparing the specification can also be a useful and cathartic exercise for yourself as you take a step back from 'business as usual' to work out what you need strategically for any person coming in.

What we do at Solve HR and what we encourage our clients to do is to consider what the overall company mission, purpose and values are in the business and have that at the top of every job description. For example, if you want to be the slickest car manufacturer "producing excellence in innovation and quality" then write that mission at the top of every job description produced. Keep it front and centre. Underneath the mission you can break this down further, for example, by stating the 'Department purpose'. For instance 'Manufacturing's mission' might in turn be to "produce quality cars efficiently to the mass market", whilst 'Quality Control's' might read "to be disciplined and diligent in robustly ensuring quality permeates the whole company working for continuous improvement". Following these statements I would also encourage you to create a section where you are prompted to enter the proposed job hours. Even if you are hesitant in defining this strictly, you can suggest the hours are flexible within parameters i.e., 'circa 25 hours' to meet the needs of the business. You can also state flexibility is a requirement of the job holder.

Keep the body of your job description simple. Itemise tasks in layman's terms. Within the personal specification outline the job competencies. Years before we might have stated the years of experience the individual is required to have in your industry or in a similar role; however, nowadays that is open to allegations of age discrimination and is best not stated in this way. In your adverts as well as your job descriptions, it is worth considering your language as there is some belief that using words like 'young, vibrant and dynamic' infers you are only seeking younger applicants and thus indirectly discriminating. If you are looking for someone to have experience, I recommend using words like 'proven', 'thorough' or other similar synonyms. For example, a 'proven competent book-keeper' or "a thorough understanding of market forces" or "in-depth referenced experience and knowledge of car manufacturing."

After looking at the experience, you should then look at detailing what IT skills and levels of proficiency you require for your role and the wider business. If you are a fairly technology advanced business, who uses Slack (a cloud-based set of proprietary team collaboration tools and services, founded by Stewart Butterfield) or other modern communication methods beyond email, then do state this. It can work both ways: some potential applicants without this skill and knowledge set may be deterred from applying, whilst others might be enthused about a company that uses these modern tools which overcomes their hesitancy about applying.

Detailing the competencies or basic behaviours you would expect the job applicants to bring to your role is also important, not only at the recruitment stage, but also later on in the employee's life in your company. If you are hiring for an accounts assistant, attention to detail might be a key requirement – thus you might state, "meticulous attention to detail". Or you may require someone with strong interpersonal skills that are confident with clients if they are in an accounts management role. Or if you are looking for a sales person you might specific evidence of 'tenacity' and follow through.

Furthermore, don't overlook 'hygiene factors' for the role. By that I mean *"factors that characterize the context or environment of a person's work"*, such as physical work environment, supervision policies or relationships with co-workers and supervisors. Lack of consideration for hygiene factors can cause issues for you and the employee and may lead to mutual dissatisfaction. For example, does the applicant need to be able to drive? Or have a car? Specify what qualifications are necessary. Consider things like having valid and up to date certificates. Or holding the right licences e.g. for practicing law or even working in a bar (the ones that sell drinks, not the ones that practice law!) Taking all of these things into account will help both you and those being hired during the screening process.

Advertising mediums.

There are many mediums available these days to advertise you have a job available. Although you have written your job description do not become confused and think that it is sufficient to post this on an online job board. You should translate your job description and personal specification, suitable for internal use, into an effective sales pitch to explain to candidates why they might want to work for you, in short a job advert. The key objective of your job advert is to attract candidates into applying.

My preferred method of advertising would be to have snappy interest-grabbing questions, asking people to self-select.

- Do you want to earn more money in sales?
- Are you a strong book keeper looking for their next career move?
- Do you love cars and always wanted to work in the industry?

After capturing an individual's attention, summarise your business. Have you won any product awards? Better still have you won any Good Employer awards? Even being a small business or new start-up can be leveraged into a powerful message, particularly for graduates who increasingly want to get involved with new ideas and concepts and be a part of the journey of growth. They may view large corporates with increasing cynicism and view the small business as having greater personal development and autonomy opportunities.

Furthermore, don't forget to give an overview of the job and tasks – they'll need to know what the work entails after all! If the role involves considerable data entry then clarify that. Coupled with your person specification being very specific about your requirements and experience. It's probably the section where you do the least selling.

Lastly, you will also need a statement or reference link on your privacy policy to ensure GDPR compliance. This is because you will be harvesting through applicants sending you their CV's personal details. GDPR refers to the General Data Protection Regulations introduced in 2018. Your policy should mentioned upfront, before a candidate sends you their information and state:

- How long you will keep their data.
- For what purpose you will use their data, for example is it exclusively for recruitment only or would you add them to a mail list (Note. you must make this clear and they should have the option to 'opt-in' rather than be automatically subscribed).
- Who the Data Controller is and how to contact them in a SME often the Managing Director.
- Where the data is held: is it in the EU or does some of it go outside of the EU borders?
- That they are entitled to exercise their rights under the General Data Protection Regulations 2018 articles 14 to 22.

If you expect to be inundated with applications, add a line at the bottom of your advert stating that due to the high level of anticipated applications you will only be in contact with individuals who are selected to move forward in the process, and give a time-frame, so if they hear nothing within that time, they can assume they've not progressed.

Many online job boards allow you to put in pre-screening questions which can help you in managing applications. These can be quite helpful because if the role does require a specific qualification, such as the ability to drive, those that don't meet your minimum requirement can be automatically screened out without clogging your inbox. Job portals often allow you to craft an automatic response that is sent to those candidates that don't meet your minimum criteria. These settings can be switched on and off depending on your role and applications.

LinkedIn.com is another great resource for finding candidates and there's a ton of information about how best to use it for that purpose. If you have a fair number of connections, you can often reach out for free to potential candidates or go in cold if you prefer. Additionally you could pay for advertising on their site – the key benefit being accurate targeting of your advert to relevant active and passive job seekers. For instance if their existing profile job title is "Customer Services Manager" they will see notifications of other Customer Services Manager job adverts. So even if they are not looking for a job, you may get candidates where a particular role or advertising company takes their fancy and motivates them to apply. It's another reason to write a compelling eye-catching advert! After all you do want the best, I presume?

Headhunting can be easy with this tool. If you know that one of your competitors has a great training programme and typically produces employees who are a great fit for your organisation you can very easily search potential candidates by company name, location and job title. If this approach works well for you LinkedIn offers a professional account that we at Solve HR use to headhunt and reach out to candidates with specific qualifications and experience.

Whilst you are looking at your advert and job description, also consider the interview process you will take the candidates through that will save both your time and theirs, yet still ensure you find the right candidate. This could be as simple as requiring candidates to submit a job-relevant statement or conducting initial screening by telephone with some standard quick questions and a script prepared. This can be particularly helpful if the role involves being on the phone a lot or interacting with the public – if a candidate doesn't present well on the phone, they probably won't face-to-face so you could rule them out. Go one better than the telephone, which can be time consuming, and use one of the many high quality video conferencing platforms. Some platforms allow candidates to answer pre-defined questions which you can watch later.

If distance is not a problem, and there are several candidates to see, consider staging an assessment centre. This enables candidates to participate in both an interview and other challenges, giving you more information about them and potentially saving time in hosting a second interview. Plan for the day carefully picking team and/or individual assessments that are relevant to the job or behaviours that you are looking for. Be upfront and clear on the assessing criteria. Consider the following ideas for an assessment centre activity:

- Ask a candidate to set a table for a five course dinner or making a certain kind of cocktail in a time fixed period. These are good activities if you are hiring for an experience supervisor or hospitality worker.
- An in-tray or 'in-email box' exercise for a PA or secretary.
- Role play whereby you or a colleague plays a disgruntled customer, this could assess customer management skills, if hiring for a customer services agent or manager.

If you opt to use an assessment centre, remember to schedule in time for a wash-up session with all the assessors. This can be a quick way to select candidates and gain agreement from multiple managers on the preferred candidates. It also can mean that in just one day you might be in a position to make job offers – always good!

To be really successful in an assessment centre or in the interview process and get as many strong candidates in one room at the same time, manage their expectations upfront. If you have blocked out some time in your diary and these are the only days you can do the interviews, make sure candidates know that and that if they can't make those dates they will not be interviewed.

Interestingly when I was in my first proper job as a recruitment agent, the first company I came across whose recruitment policy and process really opened my mind was Goldman Sachs, the investment bank. They have a strong reputation for HR; their process is to routinely ask candidates at the middle management level, to meet with 10 or even 11 different key colleagues in the company, in separate stages, before they were offered a job. I know Google had a similar requirement in their earlier stages. Sheryl Sandberg in her book 'Lean In' details the process they used to undertake and that only very few senior directors in Google were able to authorise recruitment.

The benefit of doing it like this is a check and balance on ensuring hires meet the business fit, culture, values, knowledge and experience and senior people have been bought into the hire and feel consulted and thus more likely to ensure the success of the new recruit. The process can take up to three to five weeks, unless you have planned in advance and because of this and often only works in a strong brand, where candidates really desire to work for a leading company. Otherwise unless you manage candidate's expectations up front that this is your process and the reasons why, you may lose candidates who might feel they are being made to jump too many hurdles.

As an SME owner it is very unlikely that you will have 10 people for candidates to meet with and if you did you may want to consider the impact this would have on your process, however, instead you may want to consider that family members meet with candidates who will be in a key role. When I was recruiting my first hire I asked my Father to meet with the candidates I had short listed. His perspective was good because he knows me and he knows how I work. You could also ask your accountant or a professional friend or even a recruitment agent where there is no incentive for them. In the end, I actually also used a close friend who is a recruitment agent who helped me promote my post in the market, added a bit of professionalism and credibility to the process and gave me another view on the candidates fit and suitability for my business. Particularly important in my profession.

Yes an agent might appear to be a costly outlay for an SME, however, I would also point out, getting it wrong, especially with your first hire could be even more costly. Some of the hazards include; getting someone who doesn't get your working practices or objectives, doesn't share your work ethos or passions or could even be dishonest.

Certainly getting the wrong person especially if they are a first hire can be so much more costly than taking some time and effort to get the right person. It could be the difference between accelerating your business and doubling revenue or losing half of your profit as you find yourself paying a salary and your return on this investment not paying off.

It helps to acknowledge the situation your company is in at the time of recruitment. Are you overwhelmed as a company by the volume of work? Are you struggling with a reduced workforce due to illness? Be honest when interviewing candidates. Many SME owners recruit out of knee-jerk desperation. It's very understandable. I encourage you though, to forecast as best you can when you think you might need to hire, even if that's difficult and relies upon factors such as the acquisition of a new contract.

Preparing for recruitment by speaking in advance to friends and family, fellow business owners and suppliers about upcoming vacancies can provide you with a starter pot of CVs to review when you are ready to push the button on recruiting someone. What we do at Solve HR, as many other businesses also do, is interview a candidate with a good CV, regardless of the availability of a vacancy. This way we contacts for the future in the event we acquire a larger project and we have to mobilise resources quickly.

To provide some tangible and objective evidence to differentiate between candidates it can be helpful to create a matrix to help you score candidates on some basic competency outcomes, especially if a number of candidates will be interviewed over a period of time. This objectivity can challenge your presumptions and feelings about a candidate when assessing their actual suitability for the role, helping you stay focussed on what you are looking for.

Oftentimes it can be easy to get carried away about other skills or experience a candidate might be able to bring to your business and you can then lose focus on your actual requirements as you are already looking at other possibilities; when this happens you are not wrong but be aware of what you're doing and be hard with yourself to ensure you make the right decision.

An example of a Competency Matrix:

Competency	Score
Comments/Evidence to support.	Each competency could either be scored numerically from 1 to 5 or using descriptions e.g. Poor, Unsatisfactory, Satisfactory, Very Good, Excellent
Impression/Professionalism.	
Clarity of Communication.	
Customer Service ethic.	
Evidence of flexibility.	
Team Working.	
Initiative.	
Attention to Detail.	
Sales skills.	

Top tips for recruiting the best:

1. Preparation is key: spend time scoping out a job description and a person specification.
2. Make your adverts stand out: why do I want to work for you, sell me the job!
3. Interview a number of times involving your team where possible, then listen to their feedback and follow it.
4. Let the process work: the right candidate will wait and respect your process.
5. Use behavioural analysis such as DISC or Myers Briggs Profiling, contextualising the results against your own teams' behaviours or the weaknesses so you know what a candidate can bring.
6. Use technology to support your advertising and screening where you can.
7. Cast your net wide: agencies can often get interested candidates that an SME might not normally attract; they can also handle the tricky offer stage. NOTE: negotiate fees with them, don't take their standard rates.
8. Start as you mean to continue…. Have the Contract of Employment professionally prepared and ensure any 'Offer letter' does not contradict it but clearly outlines the main terms of the employment relationship. Make sure you get two copies of the Employment Contract signed and file them safely.

9. Follow up with a thoroughly planned induction for at least the first two weeks of employment. Take some time to brain dump all of the things a new person will need to know. Start this by putting their shoes on. What will they want to know (where the nearest toilet is!)? Then think about all the systems, rules and processes they need to do a good job.

CONCLUSION

This book has aimed to give you guidance for some key employment scenarios that most SME businesses are likely to experience. There will always be many more scenarios and there will always be greater complexities associated with each than can be covered in this book – that's the nature of running a business and employing people. Solve HR Ltd, the company behind this book, can help if you find yourself needing more information.

The best way to stay free of employment disputes is to follow a great process for HR-related matters:

- Put everything in writing – if it's not in writing it didn't happen! Disciplinary meetings, redundancy situations, performance issues, contractual terms, even informal chats should be written down in clear, specific, non-accusatory language which fully explains the actions your company has taken and the joint expectations for moving forward.
- Respect employees' rights, especially that of being accompanied at meetings, and ensure the 48-hours advance notice requirement is followed so they have enough time to prepare. Where there is evidence or an investigation, make sure all that information has been supplied in advance.
- Ensure you follow up in writing with a decision and where required inform the employee of their right to appeal. You may opt to give all employees this right irrespective of the law to help pre-empt a tribunal or further issues manifesting.
- Following the steps above will ease the management of any dispute process, and if a dispute escalates to a tribunal, the evidence collected above will prove invaluable in showing you did everything you could in the dispute management process as any 'reasonable employer' would.
- Softer options to consider which can be just as useful in the long run include:
- Training relevant managers in employment matters so they have knowledge of potential pitfalls and can therefore identify and flag issues before they escalate.
- Decide on the culture you wish to encourage in your business. Be clear on your expectations for performance and yet also foster a growth culture, where mistakes can be made, then harder HR decisions should be easier when they are required.

- Keep up-to-date with industry-specific employment law changes through an advisor or your industry body as they can seriously affect your business e.g. recent case rulings on holiday pay due on commission payments and overtime has seriously affected some companies' bottom line.

The practical, legal and processual points are key to keeping you on the right side of the law; however, a major factor in ensuring that you don't end up in a tribunal irrespective of how well you follow the process, will be how you deal with people.

In a study quoted in Malcolm Gladwell's 'Blink', American insurance companies on their quest to 'risk' analyse the factors that lead to some medical doctors being sued by patients more than other doctors, found that it came down to a few main factors. The study evaluated the length of time doctors spent with their patients and the engagement they each had on social factors, such as enquiring about the patient's health, pets and grandchildren. They discovered that they could draw conclusions on the likelihood of a doctor being sued based on the 'tone' of the consultation and the average length of time the doctor took, even when the insurers were not privy to the content of the consultations. In short, their findings were that doctors that spent more time with their patients, maintaining a friendly rather than officious tone, were significantly less likely to be sued by their patients, even if their advice was deficient or poor.

Why is this relevant to this book? Hopefully it serves as a reminder to still engage with your employees in these often stressful and hurtful processes. Explain your 'why', as Simon Sinek advocates: people need to be treated with dignity and respect, but also understand the reasons for your decisions. This understanding can then help them rationalise and de-personalise a redundancy or dismissal and hopefully see the context in a bigger picture.

Good luck in your employment with people and if you need further advice please get in touch.

Stephanie
stephanie.robinson@solvehr.co.uk

About The Author

Stephanie Robinson is the founder of Solve HR Ltd. and a Chartered Member of CIPD*.

Before establishing Solve, Stephanie worked in consultancy and has many years of generalist HR experience and strong knowledge of employment Law. Customer focussed and especially on delivery, Stephanie's passion is to give the best value to our clients, minimise risk and ensure excellent service.

At the age of 17 Stephanie taught English in Tokyo for a year. While she was teaching English in a High School, she was also learning Japanese. During university, Stephanie completed an internship with the Foreign Policy Association in New York where she assisted in the organising of the annual World Leadership Forum. Her highlight was interviewing Ambassador Stalin, of the Swiss Embassy on the Swiss accession to the United Nations. After travelling around Brazil and working in the US, Stephanie started working in HR recruitment in London. Routinely recruiting for PricewaterhouseCoopers, Ernst & Young, Goldman Sachs and Accenture she developed further accounts with Johnson & Johnson and LG.

Before establishing Solve, Stephanie worked for a large UK Employment Law consultancy where she worked with a client base of over 500 developing their contracts of employment and solving their employment disputes. Prior to that Stephanie was head hunted for the role of HR Manager in a global pharmaceutical company responsible for 400 employees onsite in Bathgate, Edinburgh. There she managed a large scale redundancy project, culture change initiative and employee relations. Stephanie has experience of working within HR in Hospitality, Outsourcing, the Legal Sector and Manufacturing.

* Chartered Institute of Personnel and Development

17274245R00074

Printed in Great Britain
by Amazon